WHY WE ARE HERE ON EARTH
AND **WHAT** IS OUR **TRUE PURPOSE?**

WHAT
Can I Do?

PETER DEACON

WHY WE ARE HERE ON EARTH
AND **WHAT** IS OUR **TRUE PURPOSE?**

WHAT
Can I Do?

MEREO

Cirencester

Published by Mereo

Mereo is an imprint of Memoirs Publishing

25 Market Place, Cirencester, Gloucestershire GL7 2NX
Tel: 01285 640485, Email: info@mereobooks.com
www.memoirspublishing.com, www.mereobooks.com

First published in England, 2013

Book jacket design Ray Lipscombe

ISBN 978-1-86151-015-0

Printed in England

See more about the author and to purchase the book go to
www.communicatingwithbasics.com

Acknowledgement

I would like to thank Pauline Lelliott for correcting my errors and helping to put the book in order.

CONTENTS

In the beginning was Source

Most people have forgotten about the source of all creation. We may *think* or *believe* we never knew the real source of our existence. We have been too busy struggling to live in this world to bother about learning the truth. Who we are has never been taught in schools. Indigenous tribes around the world may have more knowledge about that than we do. It makes me wonder who the real civilised beings are.

I believe Source created its body, which we call the Universe. It contains energies that are way beyond our understanding. The Source of all creations has never appeared to us on earth in human form. Source has no reason to want to take on the shape of a human, so let's bring this idea into perspective.

You are a god on earth, made from the same energy as Source. Suppose you learned the art of creating all the fleas in the world. Would you want to appear to those fleas as one of them? I don't think so.

We could look at the mentality of humans as having the mentality of a flea in the universe. We know how to hop from one place to another, and that's all we know about life. That gives you some idea how much knowledge we have about the true reason for life. We are not as big or as clever as our egos think we are. We say we don't like wars, but we mentally argue and fight with our friends and neighbours. We are right and they are wrong. Is that creating a happy life?

Source created spirits, who gave birth to souls, who come to Earth to learn how to create experiences with love like Source.

Human bodies were originally designed by Source, yet we have the ability to change our body's shape and condition to match our desires. All this is connected to evolution. I have only a small understanding of the way evolution works. Most of our understanding is done through guesswork, or how we *imagine* things to be.

Source and your higher self, the one who gave birth to you, know everything about spirit matters, because that is who they are. They never enter Earth's atmosphere or get involved in Earth's duality.

A different type of energy is being filtered down to Earth from a group of stars called Aquarius. The purpose is to help us improve our personal learning process. After we were born we had to train this animal we have as a body to do the things we desire, which are different to its built-in animal instincts. Now we are to teach it to go beyond its comfort zone, beyond its animal instincts. We have learned the fighting bit that all kids go through; now we are to get sensible and start following our true loving nature.

You see, as children we had to realise that fighting each other does not create good friends. We had to learn that all people are different, and we have to accept that. There are no top dogs in this world, but there are many with big egos who *think* they are top dogs. You met them first in your school playground. Those people do not lead you, they try to control you. You should have learned by now to stay clear of them for your own safety.

The Aquarian energy is making this change as gentle as possible in your life. Don't do what I did some 40-odd years ago. I insisted on knowing what life is all about, and I used plenty of rage in stating that. I had been asking that question for 25 years and never once did I get an answer, or rather never once did I stay around long enough to listen to it.

This time the reply came back with the same force as my rage, but in a loving way. The answer appeared as three pinpricks which looked like an upside-down triangle stuck near the ceiling at the top of my house. There were no words, but that picture frightened the living daylights out of me. I rushed down to my body and hid in it for quite a few days.

The picture of that triangle never left me. It took me another four years before I understood its meaning.

Top left dot = Knowledge. Top right dot = Responsibility. Bottom dot = Control. When you are given knowledge, you must take responsibility for it and bring the awareness of that knowledge under your control. This then represents your 'Awareness'. All this needs to be done mentally before you bring that knowledge down to earth and ask your body to create the actions.

YOUR PERSONAL UNIVERSE

Imagine this picture. When you look at the Universe in a clear sky, imagine you are looking at a living organism held together by energy. There are energy links between suns, solar systems, galaxies and so forth which I imagine as the cells, organs and glands forming what I call the Energy Body of Source.

Your personal universe is formed in the same way, by all the cells which make up your body. Your body is a microcosm of the macrocosm in the sky. This is the closest you ever get to see the 'Creator of All there Is' and the closest your cells ever get to seeing you. The cells in your body are the creators of your body. The blueprint of your body was created by Source and your body was tuned in to the energies of the macrocosm the moment you arrived in your mother's body. The energies needed to implement your programme for coming to earth were gradually tuned into your body's cells by the stars. This was done slowly as your body's electrical energy system was gradually wired up.

At the precise time your body took its first breath (when you were born), it was again tuned into more energies of the cosmos. The program it tuned into this time was the one you planned with your HS (Higher Self) prior to arrival. Source connected you up to your personal frequency, so now you have your own radio station. You can tune in and check out your pre-planned mission any time you like, but you only get the next bit that needs to be accomplished. This is because your HS is in charge of the station.

You have the ability to communicate with your HS at any

time, especially when you meet difficulties concerning your actions on earth. It communicates with you constantly, answering your questions and sending you the information you need to know concerning your mission and the safety of your body.

Your HS puts objects and people in your space that are connected to your reason for being here. At times HS puts objects and people on your road which seem to block you from arriving at your chosen destination of the day.

There are many reasons why this is done. Maybe you are unknowingly heading into someone else's disaster area. You may need to ask your HS why you are being blocked. All these situations are pieces of your jigsaw puzzle which help you to form the life you have pre-planned to live here.

Nature also plays its part in your game of life. Your HS offers you suggestions which help you to learn to create your purpose every second of your life. It also does its best to steer you away from harm. Remember you are in charge of all your actions on earth. Your HS will do nothing for you. It accepts your status as being a learning god in your own right.

To make the subject of pre-planning better for you to understand; you never go on holiday without first planning where you intend to go and what you intend to do when you get there. The same applied when you decided to pay Earth a visit. I am talking about you the Soul. It may be difficult for you to accept this if you still believe there is only the body.

You acquire knowledge as you move through life from two places. Energy from the Universe is flowing into your body via our solar system. The planets in our solar system are the people speaking to you on your TV station in picture form. They are broadcasting the information you need to know at the time you need to know it. This information reminds you of the mission you set in motion prior to coming here. This is the way we receive encouragement and ideas concerning our pre-chosen purpose.

As an earth body you may say that is your intuition. But you Soul know this is your Inner Tuition.

Your body is made up of living cells. A single cell is a complete energy unit in its own right and you are its god. Each cell has the ability to receive and send energy to all other cells in your body and to its chakra points. Each chakra point is a specialised energy centre that deals with and stores a certain type of energy. Chakra 2 stores your actions; 3 your emotions; 4 your feelings (loving, I hope). Chakra 5 stores your communications; and Chakra 6 your visions or pictures.

These special areas send personal information about you out into space. And they also send and receive information from any body in your space and any space you have your attention on.

The cells in your body are the stars in your Universe. The chakra points are your galaxies, which automatically send out the message about your life experiences so Source and other Souls (with or without bodies) can receive this information.

Remember you are only able to do all this when you own an Earth body, so your body is a radio station broadcasting to the world and the universe. How do you think you know what someone is thinking? You pick up their energy, of course.

Haven't you ever wondered how some people can pick up

your thoughts and feelings and how Source receives your information?

HARD HITTING

As I said before, my mum used to gently tap me on the top of the head and say 'You've got a brain of yer own, why don't yer use it'? So I'm going to tap you lightly on the head with a few hard hitting questions:

■ Have you forgotten who you are and where you came from?

■ Can you not see the point in keeping your physical body as healthy as possible?

■ Have you stopped creating your own life?

■ Are you following the dreams of others?

■ Have you made your body so mentally and/or physically weak that you now expect others to do everything for you?

Nasty questions, aren't they? Be honest with yourself. How much effort are you actually putting in to create your life the way you want it to be? If you just said 'very little', then:

■ Are you unable to see any higher than the ground you walk on?

■ Do you see or accept another as your Master?

■ Do you use pound signs as your symbol of motivation to find a way to live in this world?

- Is your main desire to get more money in life?
- Do you rely mostly on your Ego attitude?

Regrettably I must conclude that in the majority of so-called civilised humans, we have to answer 'yes' to most of these questions.

None of this is your fault. Our ancestors inadvertently set this way of life in motion for us. They were learning what we should not do in life and mistook it to mean what we should do, so they taught us the ego way of living. We also quickly found it easier to follow someone else than to use our own brains. We chose the easy way out by follow what we call our leaders. Unfortunately it didn't lead us out of anything; it just ploughed us deeper into the mire. We need to do our own thinking and make up our own mind about what we want to do and where we want to go.

WE NEED TO CHANGE

Thank goodness you have found this book and found who you are, and thank goodness you still have your power of choice. It may be a little rusty but it is still in perfect working order.

To be different takes effort on your part. It is wise to listen to those who you *feel* know more about what is happening in the world. If the things they are saying match your reality of life, then allow them to be your guide. Continue doing your own thinking within the boundaries of what they say and you should make it safely into being your own Master.

We have been asking for help for a long time, and our

request has been answered in the form of Aquarian energy. Aquarius is pouring out its knowledge, for the benefit of those who desire to use it. This is a different way of sending us knowledge. The old way was the slabs of stone Moses brought down from the mountain. Gee, I bet his arms ached. Only a few could read those stones. In this modern age everyone is tune into the energies of Aquarius, whether they listen to and use those energies or not.

We are slowly learning how to use this new energy by choosing experiences we would like to create, and willing to learning from their outcome. Well! Sometimes we learn from what we have done, and sometimes we learn from what we are actually doing right now.

AN OUTCOME

This is the effect our physical body or verbal action created.

It is the effect our action has on another or others.

We have learnt how to share our knowledge with each other electronically; that's the same way Source shares its knowledge with us. (More about that later.)

We can as 'People of the World' work as a team and make Planet Earth a better place to live on. We have a lot to learn and we will get a lot wrong whilst learning. Just like in school, we got more sums wrong than we got right in the beginning. As our awareness grew we got the hang of it, we learned how to correct our mistakes and get good results.

When you learn how to reach out and work with the knowledge of Source your life changes; you feel the difference in your body, and those good feelings also strengthen your confidence.

Let's try to bring back and convert the 'We are all one' crowd.

It is time to put actions into your beliefs. Let's all work at it as a team of individuals. Let's all start living forward and stop living backwards (that's eviL, remember). Let's all work and help each other to lift our energies up so we all (as a group of individuals) rely on the advice of Source. Let's all work as a team to get it right this time by using our personal power of choice. Learn to say 'No' with a smile on your face to those things that don't feel right for you. Then let that 'not feel good thing' go and its energies will no longer bother you. You will learn how to do that later.

First you need to build your confidence and prove to your Self that you are the 'Soul' attached to your body. You have to prove to yourself that you are a God on Earth, who is equal to and as capable as all the other Soul gods on Earth.

Top Dogs are only Souls who have more awareness and knowledge in specialised subjects. Use these Top Dog Souls as your teacher if their subject matter is connected to your reason for being here.

GUIDELINES

On Earth your body has to follow Earth rules. You Soul are guided by spirit energy. To create an experience you have to be balance in both worlds at the same time, or you will end up creating a mistake. That means you will have to create that action again, (like in film making) but more balanced next time.

MORE ABOUT SOUL TRAVEL

This may sound strange, but we as Souls often travel without our body, especially when our body is busy creating a boring repetitive experience.

Our brain is a wonderful instrument, yet we know very little about its workings. After we learn something, that information is stored somewhere so we don't have to learn the same things over and over again. Life gets very boring when repeating repetitive actions, so we say 'Hooray! Now my body is doing this I can shoot off to a place I have my attention on.' We are always space travelling, it's a part of our nature. We opt out of observing what our body is doing and go walkabout. Nobody said you have to stay with your body all your life. If we couldn't Soul Travel that would make a mockery of 'being a free Spirit'.

The down side of Soul Travel is, if you are not accepting responsible for your body; you leave the door open for accidents to happen to it.

There is a time and a place to safely Soul Travel - which is at any time in any place when your body is not in motion or communicating with another. You will be surprised how many people Soul Travel while having a conversation.

Here is an example of no communication.

You and your friend are in town on a shopping spree, and she, looking at a wedding dress in a shop, says 'Sally got married last Saturday and they have gone to Ibiza for their honeymoon. I have always wanted to go to Ibiza, have you been there?' You said 'Shall we eat in the Italian restaurant today?' That didn't answer your friend's question, did it?

When your friend mentioned the key word **Honeymoon**, you shot off (Soul travelled) to Italy, which happens to be where you had a wow of a time on your honeymoon. The food was good too. Then you came back, and as food was on you're mind you asked your question.

Your friend thinks you never answer her questions; it's a waste of time talking with you. So you loose a few brownie points in the eyes of your friends because you do this often.

GETTING INTO PT

A quick way to do this is to:

1. First take a deep belly breath. This fills your body with more life-giving oxygen than your lungs can possibly hold.
2. Hold for a second, and feel this energy race through your body down your arms to your hands, as maybe a tingling sensation.
3. As you breathe out, physically relax all your muscles and *know* you are relaxing them.
4. Take another deep belly breath and as you breathe out, know that you are here in your body, in this present moment ready to do what you intend to do or say.
5. Now breathe normally and create the action.

Knowing you're here in this present moment ready to do something or say something is the important part. Some call this 'being in the zone'. That, to me, is stating an incomplete sentence. 'Being in the zone' may cause problems as it means you can be in any zone you like. That doesn't mean you are here in your body right now. So get into the area where your body is right now.

Your body is always in PT and its zone is right HERE. Don't try to complicate the system by incorporating other ancient systems. We are living in modern times following modern updates created through evolution of our mind, so keep it as simple as possible. We don't need to light candles, we use electricity now. I bet you forgot that the ancients lit candles to see where they were going and what they were doing. We love altering the meaning of those things we don't fully understand.

If something distracts you before doing something, know it is a natural survival habit called curiosity. If your eyes can't see it, it may cause you to leave your body and go and see what is causing the distraction. There you go; you've gone Walk-About again. So remove all distractions from your space and know you are with your body. I prefer to call this state being in Present Time. It is the safest place and frame of mind to be in before creating any mental, verbal or physical action.

TWO SIMPLE EXERCISES

Imagination is a wonderful tool, which proves you are the Soul in control of your body.

FUN EXERCISE 1

Sit on a chair, close your eyes and imagine you are sitting about 12 inches away from a window and with your back to it. Imagine two hooks in the ceiling with a rope draped from these hooks holding a comfortable seat in the middle. It looks like a swing.

Now imagine yourself sitting on that swing facing into the room. Start swinging back and forth; swing out through the window, until you can see the outside wall. Keep swinging harder and harder and look for different details on the outside wall each time you swing out. What colour is it? What else can you see on that wall? This is fun; you may even feel the motion of swinging in your belly area.

When you feel you have had enough fun, Stop.

When using your imagination, know you created the whole scenario and your body added feeling to it as a bonus. Your body's emotions are always connected to those things you create and see as a Soul Being. You were actually looking at that outside wall. Go outside and see how many details you saw were correct. When talking with your HS the things you see with your imagination are not *created* by you.

Nothing in this world is perfect. Soul's vision is different from the vision your body eyes have, but they both reflect the energy they sense into your pineal gland, where that gland deciphers and translates that energy into an Earth-reality movie. Colours may be more vivid and details clearer in Soul picture, or if you have doubts when doing this, then your pictures may appear fuzzy due to the blocking doubt energy.

There are none as blind as those Souls who do not wish to

see. Whatever you saw, know only you Soul saw it and it was your body that added the sensations to it. Well done.

If you can still remember that experience, then you also know you created that reality moment by moment; your cells recorded everything. It is now your truth, which takes this experience beyond just being 'My Reality'.

FUN EXERCISE 2
THE ART OF CREATING ENERGY LINKS

Nothing in this world is difficult unless you choose to make it so. Listening to your left brain's mind causes that.

As Earth beings: if you wanted to say something to someone, you put your attention on them. When you get their attention (sometimes we call their name), when you see they are looking at you, you then use the energies of **desire** and **determination** and say your message.

As a Soul being; when you mentally put your attention on someone who is not in your space (that means they are not standing beside you), you create an image of that person and this image is the energy link which acts as your telephone line. Actually, you Soul go down that energy line into their space. Now '*think*' a loving message to them, as youngsters in love do. Sometimes that person you put your attention on contacts you.

THINKING ABOUT SOMEONE

Have you ever wondered why we suddenly start thinking about someone? One of two things causes this:

1. That person was thinking of you at that time and you tuned into their energy. If you were to phone them after it happened, they may say they were just thinking about you and you phoned. Wow!
2. Or something in your space reminded you of that person. A photo, a song, a colour, just anything.
3. This thought may also have come from your HS for some reason. Dwell on it for a minute and see if there is any more information connected to it. Then either take action, or let it go.

You may say or think '*I hope they are all right*'. If you thought that, then yes that energy most probably came from your *Mind*. Your *Mind* only draws your attention to the down side of life. Why would you think they were not all right?

Some people speak their message into thin air (without first creating an energy link to a person or spirit being), so the receiver will not know you were talking to them. It's very doubtful that a stranger will pick up or listen to your message, because it did not have their signature, or 'bar code', attached.

So it is wise to create an energy link first by putting our attention on the person you intend to send your message to. Your attention doesn't have to follow the directions of a road map to find where they are, or live. Spirit energy doesn't follow Earth rules.

If you wish to communicate with a Spirit in the Spirit Realm, or a physical person not in your space, the same rule applies. You as Soul just need to think of that person and put your attention on the image you have of them and you will be where they are. Their physical body's actual location plays no part in this.

You don't have to move your body around to locate their direction, or rely on a map and compass to find them. Working as a Soul Being, whatever you want to know or whoever you want to see is always right in front of you. Everything is in a straight line, right in front of your eyes.

With Earth objects, energy doesn't bend round corners. Put a radio mast behind a mountain and you won't pick up the signal the other side of the mountain. Working as a Soul being, the rules are different.

Young lovers are good at using this ability. They are so much in love with each other, which means they are using their natural love to the full. This causes them to make silly mistakes in their body space because each goes walkabout to where the other is, when they should be with their body. Some people, who have been there themselves, know what is going on and say 'I think they are in love'. If the lovers don't know who they really are, then they miss the important lessons attached to these feelings. Your body always knows when you are soul travelling.

LET'S PUT SOUL TRAVEL TO THE TEST

Your HS is not located inside your body and it has never come to Earth. The only Spirit allowed inside your body is *you Soul.*

HS can be found wherever you *feel* it is in a straight line. You have to create your own image of how you would like you're 'High Self' to look.

Only you are capable of giving your body Life. When you decide you have completed your mission, your body goes back to the earth, and you go home, wherever that is.

We do not have all the knowledge of Source in our body. We only store the knowledge of those things we enquire about and the actions we have physically or verbally created (or not) that support that fact. Most people look up to the heavens if they want to talk to their maker, and that's a good place to start so close your eyes.

Now you know you are the Soul, you will notice you can see just as clearly with your eyes closed as you can when they are open. Some people think they can see more clearly by using the third eye (located on the forehead just above the bridge of the nose). This we call our Spiritual eye. This eye is the place your Body uses to see the images of where you are as they form in space.

You Soul do not use this eye to see. You are not governed by earth time, so you know exactly where you are all the time.

Some people are so left minded they don't believe this is possible, they are afraid to go to the place where they can see images. Yet that doesn't stop them from visualising all the time about things like: 'What are we going to have for dinner today'? Okay clever clogs, what food did you imagine and how did you see that food?

Becoming more aware of what you are doing is an important thing here. As your attention is on your HS at this moment, then whatever you *imagine* your HS looks like, that is the image you are seeing right now. Your HS is always there. It never goes walkabout.

The information you *mentally* request may appear in front of you. Sometimes HS disappears and pictures form. But that doesn't have to be the only way 'Inner-Tuition' appears to you. People are different, so find out how mental information arrives in your brain.

You have just reconnected your side of the two-way energy link to your HS. The side from HS to you was never broken. HS has always been with you trying to get your attention, trying to instruct or direct you all your life. It's only your side of the communication line that went dead after you mentally turned it off, after you refused to remain in contact.

Now for a giggle, go and sit on your HS' lap; the true meaning of Father Christmas still exists. Every gift you receive on Earth comes via your HS.

Go sit on your HS lap and allow your body to use all its senses to feel the softness and love, and be really loving. HS has done its best to look after you ever since before you were a nipper, so thank your HS for always being there for you and for trying to help you (even though you didn't listen to what it said most of the time). Your HS has always loved the body you created. HS knows no other *Feeling*, and has no material body to love of its own. That reality never changes.

You may wonder why I say 'HS loves your body' and not 'loves you'! When two equal energies of love meet, neither can boost the other; they are both the same polarity and both perfect loving machines, so nothing happens. They cancel each other out. This is why your HS cannot control you, even if it wanted to. But your body needs all the love it can get, so HS sends it all the love it has to help it to stay healthy and perform properly for you. Your body in this world is a miracle-in-progress.

When you are with your HS your body has no intention of missing out on this experience. All cells in your Right Brain tune into these feeling of love and uses it to heal its energy systems. Just notice how your body feels right now.

You need your body in order to feel these sensations of love from HS. These are the same kind of feeling you should be sending to others. Compare it with the kind of love you do send to others. Your Mind sends Love to others with 'Yer but' and 'If only' attached to them.

Your body may feel slightly overwhelmed with joy or slightly weepy at this point, especially if it hasn't felt this good for a long time or if you have been accidentally-on-purpose neglecting it or misusing it. Food energises your body, it does not make your body feel happy; only love does, and the way you lovingly get it to perform your actions.

Well done! You have remade your connection to HS. You are back with the energy of life. Now you are free to move away from the fear of death, and start having fun by creating more life giving actions with your body.

If you would like to create your life differently from how it is right now, then ask your HS about something you would like to create. But this time stay there and listen to the reply.

My mum used to say to me when I asked her something a dozen times 'Why don't you listen?' I never did listen to her answer, I was always too busy thinking about or doing something else. My mum never taught me how to get or stay in PT to listen to her answer or how to talk to my HS.

I found the reason why 50 years later. Her body had many battle scars through various operations and she didn't think it was as perfect as it should be and didn't think she would be allowed into heaven. After a nice cuppa and a short chat she felt a lot happier and knew she was perfect. My mum thought she was just a body, so she didn't know how to chat with her HS, so she wasn't able to teach me that when I was young.

To chat with your HS you need to get this formula right.

First you have to relax and let the outer world (Earth) go: Know you are in this present moment and move into your Right Brain as you stay in present time. (Don't tune into your Mind or this whole action will not work).

Now tune in to your HS and ask your question, then listen for, and to, the reply.

'Thanks Mum, it took me quite a few years before I got the hang of doing this! OK Mum, so only a few people had this knowledge in your days and you weren't one of them. Got it?

HS doesn't always speak to you in words, it speaks to you in energy vibrations which may or may not sound like words to you.

Your body has the ability to receive a conglomeration of energies and feelings all coming through the pipeline at the same time, arriving at your pineal gland. It wouldn't surprise me if you knew what is being said anyway, so just rely on your body's feelings. Your body's cells are always tuned into the incoming energy from around your space and from your HS.

Your cells worship you and send out tracker beams to follow you wherever you go. They listen in to your conversations and feel good or bad - depending on what they hear - and how the energies being sent out are vibrating.

This is also how you get to know the things that feel right for your body to create; your body always tells you if it feels capable or not capable of doing something.

Tune into your body's feelings every time you are not sure about something and follow what it says. Otherwise you are showing little respect for it and not using it to the best of its ability. Remember - you are supposed to be working as a team.

If there is something you are creating you are not sure of or still don't fully understand, then ask HS some more questions about it right now. You always have time to talk to your HS. It only takes a few seconds to do and you always have time to listen to the reply. Rushing things is just a bad Earth habit. Your conversation may take milliseconds, so why are you always in so much of a hurry to do nothing afterwards?

Enjoy all that you feel while with your HS; it often throws in a few bonuses for good measure, like making you smile and feel proud about yourself. Stay in present time, be aware and enjoy it all.

Being with HS is the only place you can sense true pleasure in your life. It shows you feel-good-to-do movies before you decide to bring them down to Earth to create them. You can create many good things by practising this system.

Some people think that once they have stored the information HS just gave them, that's the end of the story. They never put it into practice. Others think they have reached the end of this cycle of action and wander round like walking encyclopaedias. If you don't use this information, you will be full of useless knowledge and you might as well be a robot for the good it's going to do you.

I have said this because I have tried the zombie route and it wasn't a pleasant feeling. Drugs and alcohol can get you into zombie mode much faster than the way I got there, so I suggest you don't go there. There is no fun there and the world is still the way you left it when you come back.

CYCLES OF ACTION FOR CHANGE

Living is all about being in charge of your life, being in present time (PT) and creating the experiences you desire to get an outcome from to the best of your ability. Oh! I almost forgot to mention; your body creates the experience for you. So do your best to create your experiences in a way that pleases and satisfies your body's comfort zone without putting it under too much stress. Should you create an experience that upsets your body, its cells get grumpy and out of balance. They may get stressed to the point of feeling ill at ease, or they may become dis-eased. The actions and thoughts you create are the cause of your body's dis-ease.

To improve anything in your life you must first have a desire to want something to be different from the way it is right now, and the only things you can make different are the ways you create your experiences.

To change an unpleasing experience:

- Close your eyes and put your attention on the experience you created that upset you.

- Love is the only energy you own. What actions did you create physically, verbally or through your thoughts that did not come up to your expectation or contain love? This will have caused some physical or mental discomfort in your body. There may have been no love in any of the three areas of that scenario.

- Do you know what actions you need to create to rectify that situation? If yes, then create those actions, and put your wrong to right.

- Life is not about 'how right you are', it's about 'how loving you are' and 'how willing you are' to allow others to live their life their way.

- If you haven't a clue how to correct the error, then get into PT. Know you are here and not still at the place the error happened. The best way to do that is by going into your right brain area by simply saying 'I am there'. This gets you out of your body's mind.

- Now put your attention on your body and relax it by slow deep belly-breathing until it feels calm. Relax your muscles on each out-breath through the mouth. This I call mental massage. You are removing tension from all cells in your body helping the pain to release.

- When this is done, visualise, or know, you are with your HS and ask:

'*How can I create (the experience) without causing pain to my body and to other people*'?

Your *Imagination* will kick in, and if you are willing to look, your HS will show you maybe a few ways to reshape that experience. Choose a way that *feels good*. Your body tells you which way it would like to do it. Then bring that knowledge out of the mental stage of the right mind and give it to your body to put it into action. Only by applying that knowledge on Earth, through the help of your body, will that experience become an earth reality. Only then does it become *your* reality.

If after applying it you find you have more questions, then go back and talk with your HS some more. There is always more to learn from the way we act out our experiences. Perfection is not possible, but that shouldn't stop you from aiming for it.

Dark energies are heavy; they cannot fly, so they sink to the bowels of the Earth from whence they came. If you want more proof, then what happens when you put a light on in a dark room? What happens to the darkness? Where did that dark energy go? It is still there, but you can no longer see it and it cannot affect you while it is in the light.

There is a way to remove dark energies which are causing pain in your body. Imagination is a powerful tool. You actually put that dark energy into your body. It belongs to one of your beliefs that is flowing against your truth. That dark energy didn't want to go into your body in the first place. So by using your imagination, you can send it out of your body just as fast.

- Imagine this painful energy as being a lot of beautifully-coloured butterflies.
- Put a window in your skin where you feel the pain.
- Open the window and tell these beautiful butterflies to leave your body right now.
- Watch the coloured butterflies fly off into the world, feeling free again.
- On each in-breath, draw in all these butterflies from around the pain area.
- On your out-breath, watch them fly away.
- Repeat this process until all the butterflies have gone, the pain area feels healthy, and you feel it is done.
- Most important of all, know you have released them.

You see, we are good natured at heart. As a matter of fact the dark energies in your body hate being there. Your body is trying to increase its power of light, so these dark energies dislike being in there, and are happy when you ask them if they want to leave and happier when you release them. Now everyone is happy.

When you have created an experience which you are not satisfied with, always ask your HS for a better way to create that experience, and options will appear. Rely on your body's feeling to tell you the way it would like to create the experience. Then ask your body to create that experience when you are ready.

You are about to get involved in some physical action now.

Before creating any experience, move into the Now (PT), know you are here, work out what you intend your body to do or say, then create that physical or verbal action as mentally planned. Remember, talking to another or to your body is also creating an experience. So do it lovingly. Using your imagination is not mad – but those who don't use it are.

DISTRACTION AND CURIOSITY

When another distracts us, we switch our attention from what we are doing to what they are doing. Sometimes we blame them for distracting us.

If a noise distracts us, we sometimes choose to find out what is creating that noise, so again we move away from what we are doing or saying to investigate.

When you learn how to stay in Present Time, and keep your attention on what you are doing or saying, then nothing will distract you. You are allowing everything to be the way it is without thinking you must be a part of it.

I was giving a talk to a few hundred people when suddenly two televisions (one behind me and the other on the side) came to life, blaring out rock and roll music. Then a flood of water appeared from the ceiling, creating a beautiful waterfall about five feet away from the audience. The noise was terrific. It was impossible to continue with my talk, so I said 'would anyone like to rock with me'? A woman stood up and was coming over to dance. I was falling into the mood of the moment then I remembered I was supposed to be giving a talk and had to call for help.

It took the electrician and plumber 15 minutes to put the scenery back to normal. The electrician kept saying 'These televisions are switched off at the mains, I don't know what is going on'. Spirit works in funny ways sometimes.

I really appreciated that woman who got up to dance with me. I got the impression she accepted life the way it is like me, and was willing to change track at a moment's notice. I loved it. I think she was the woman who said 'it was nice to see you practising what you were saying'. Go with the flow, let it all happen. And it did.

THE VALUE OF COMMUNICATION

The two most important things you need to do in this life are:

1. Keep your body breathing comfortably.
2. Be knowingly aware of things in your space.

We often think we know best and can do it alone until it all goes wrong big time. That kind of experience brings you back into Present Time in a hurry. You feel you have hit rock bottom.

As you didn't know about your HS, you may have felt quite empty and lost. You may have felt there was no one to talk to and there was nothing good in the future for you. That's how we create the downward spiral feelings of *despair, not good enough, hopelessness* etc. But you were never left alone. Your HS did its best to attract your attention even though you had broken your contact with it.

Earlier you may have had various feelings in the back of your mind, or in the pit of your stomach, that indicated you were heading in the wrong direction. You hoped it was not a truth, yet you did nothing to look deeper at the cause of these feelings; you just pressed on with your dream. You didn't even want to think about it going wrong.

Maybe you were stuck in some fantasy creating a false reality, and only came back to Earth when you heard words like 'You're fired', or some other message that brought you down to Earth in a hurry.

You should feel quite pleased that you now know who is in charge of your life. You should feel quite pleased that you have reconnected to your HS. At last you have someone sensible to talk to and help you out of any sticky situation.

Some people become spiritually aware after their body has been confined, after their way of living has come to a halt. It gives them time to think more deeply about their life, what they have done and what they haven't done. They may have been warned many times by their HS that they were heading in the wrong direction, but they ignored all help from the Spirit Realm. Just like the man in that earlier story (Book 1), who fantasised on being a manager in the firm he decided to work for. There are many ways we are forced to 'come to our senses' and I mean that in a pleasant way. We are forced to look at how we *approach* things. We are forced to look at the emotions we use. So let's get scientific.

Our scientists have come close to seeing a Soul Being, yet they are completely baffled by its presence. I am talking about quantum physics here. There are energy particles in your cells that refuse to obey our scientific Earth rules. They pop in and pop out whenever they feel like it. They are completely uncontrollable, just as Souls are. I wonder if our real opposites are the free radicals which reside in our body. We know what damage free radicals can do to the cells in our body. They appear to be as mindless as we are mindful. Yet they also know exactly what they are doing. They are just waiting to pounce on our mistakes and gobble up our weakened cells. They act like mosquitoes attracted to stagnant water. Are they just scavengers clearing away dead material from our body? If so, then they do have a good purpose and it looks like Source has thought of everything.

As I have often said – everything comes in threes.

In a way, a single cell is a miniature universe in itself.

Let's say this cell has a proton which represents the positive energy being fed to it from Earth. Earth's energy increases our body's physical strength so it can create our actions.

This cell also has a neutron which tunes into the energy we receive from the *Right Mind*. Spirit energy creates uplifting feelings in our body. Every cell in our body knows beforehand when it is about to create a good survival action by the way the scenario we chose from HS makes it *feel*.

A cell also has an electron, which is the radio link that communicates with:

1. You the soul through feelings.
2. All the other cells in your body.

An electron in your cell acts like a mini radio transmitter and receiver. Cells know which are positive or negative energies inside their body space and which kind of energies are in the immediate outside space called Earth.

All your cells work as a team to keep your body healthy. They create the universe called your body. So I have been wondering - is an electron the Spirit in a cell? Your cells rely on a higher god which is you the Soul, before they create an action. They follow your instructions to the last detail to create your desire on Earth.

Now here is where the system starts to break down a bit. This is where it starts to go wrong. You Soul have this bad habit of going walkabout. You keep disappearing to a location you have your attention on, which is away from where your body is. If a non-survival energy suddenly threatened your body verbally (such as someone with a loud aggressive voice) or physically (something or someone in your environment whose thoughts or actions are threatening your body's survival), your body may jump suddenly. Your cells immediately look for you to find out what to do next. When they can't find you, they panic and mentally go in to the Mind's movie library, looking for any past experience that solved an experience similar to the threat outside. When they find something they react accordingly, with Ego happily creating the actions. This reacting may put your body into more trouble, as your body may not be sending out the 'loving, holier-than-thou' side of your nature. Maybe the language it uses is frowned upon by others or your fist was directed right at someone's nose.

Through this reactive action, you may have just made an enemy of a friend through your body's verbal or physical behaviour. We love to blame Ego when things like this happen, but this is unfair. Ego is too thick to know what is going on, it only follows instruction on how to create body actions. Ego doesn't care who gives it instructions - you Soul, your body's cells, some other person or your reactive negative mind. As long as Ego is still alive at the end of the experience, it couldn't care two hoots. Ego only thinks of its own survival.

You don't have to wait until you hit some catastrophe before you wake up. At the back of your mind your gut feelings know when you are heading in the wrong direction. Getting things wrong and not correcting your errors is the reason your body has problems.

Many people are now moving in the right direction, and doing a wonderful job putting their message over to those who desire to know. If you care about being here then you need to make sure you really know you are the Soul Being operating that body. It must be your belief. It must mean more to you than just saying the magic words to sound popular with your friends.

Nothing is Ego's fault. We just love pointing our finger and blaming someone or something for creating our screw-ups. All Ego does is to go in to your Left Mind to find an answer when you have gone walkabout. That mind contains all the memories of your past experiences and more. Ego has no other place to get information from when you go walkabout.

Now here comes the crunch bit - When you are with your body it is you who chooses to go to your Left Mind for information concerning all things. It is you who have forgotten who you are and where you came from. It is you who have forgotten how to connect with your HS, so stop blaming ego. OK - I've had my moan, so let's move on. Don't worry, I was smiling when I said that.

I have shown you some of the things that prove you are the Soul. And that your HS is always there to help you. Now we need to get down to some real basics. What is the most important thing you have on Earth that takes you everywhere?

No it's not your car, it's your body. You need to respect it and bring it up to a reasonably healthy condition so it has the strength to create the experiences you desire. As with a car, it's a complete waste of time trying to create experiences using a weak, worn-out faulty body.

CLEAN-UP TIME

Its clean-up time folks. We have all been playing on this stage called Earth, so let's grab a broom and start cleaning up the mess we have created. It's easier and more fun to make a mess than it is to clear it up. Just ask any child. It is time to stop following your L Mind and your Earth Masters and start living life as the true identity you are. So make up your mind now to take back your control.

Use your imagination and come into Present Time (PT) and know you are in your body. Go into your Right Brain and locate the door. This is the pulsing soft spot seen on a baby's head. This is the door you use to leave your body and talk to your HS in the Spirit Realm. Your clean-up job will be much easier to achieve with the help of your HS.

You may come to realise that your Left Mind is not the only chatterbox. You may find you do your fair share of thought-talking and question-asking. You will also need Ego's help to create your actions, as there is nobody else in your body to create them for you. Your body is the feeling machine of all your experiences. If your body is feeling happy, then you love who you are *being* and what you are *doing*, so keep creating those good actions.

If you are feeling sad or down right now, then your body is

not impressed with who you are *being* or what you are *doing* or thinking right now, so get ready to cleaning up your mess by being the Soul you really are.

What thoughts are pulling you down? Take a good look at those negative thoughts. They are never going to make you happy, even saying or doing those negative things to yourself or to another will not make you happy. So make up your mind to release all that negativity right now. You want good *feeling* back in your body.

YOUR TWO MASTERS

Master No. 1

Your (Left Brain's) MIND is one of your Masters in life. You allow this mind's energies to dictate and control you. You allow it to dictate without giving its commands a second thought, or questioning why you should do that. Most of the beliefs in that mind belong to other people. Those beliefs have nothing to do with your life. These imaginary scenarios tell you how other people make their life work according to their reality, hopefully connected to their mission for being here.

Master No. 2

This is any person to whom you give permission to control your life. You allow them to tell you what to do. From their point of view, you are there to create their life experience only. Their reality of life is different to yours; they do not know about your feelings or care about your mission for being here. They just want you to do things their way. They want you to give them peace of mind by doing what they say without causing them any hassle. You may get the feeling you are nothing but their slave. Some of those beings may even be your closest friends.

Using your HS for advice does not make HS your master. Your HS has the ability to go to the powerhouse of knowledge created by Source and get knowledge about any subject you enquire about. Your HS offers you suggestions only, showing you different ways to solve your situation. You still have to choose which way you intend to go. HS respects that you are a child learning to be like God. HS never gives you orders.

Earth-bound masters are a different breed. They are people who know their subject well. You could be with one for years as they direct you along the path of your choice, containing knowledge you are interested in, knowledge which allows you to gain more awareness of the subject. When you reach the end of the course you leave.

Our earthbound masters have the ability to use their energy positively to help you, or negatively to help themselves. Only you know which way you are being directed by the Master of your choice.

You can change your masters at will. They may be someone you look up to and try to imitate. You may work for them on a friendly basis. If you choose to work for them and they allow you to use your personal skills and abilities your way, then everybody is happy. If on the other hand your master insists you do everything their way you may get the *feeling* they are using you and you are there purely to satisfy their needs. If you cannot trust them for help and support as agreed, then there is some form of imbalance. This master may drag you down into feelings of pure uselessness or pure hell, especially if you refuse to abide by their demands.

You are here to show the only energy you possess, and that is love. You are here to create all your experiences with love. So let's see how you fair when you try creating a personal relationship. I picked relationships because a loving relationship is the first thing we create in life after we were born. There are no instruction books on how to create a perfect relationship. We are all different, so we all had to work it out our own unique way, and we all succeeded.

WHAT CAN I DO?

To answer that question you really have to go mental.

Nothing can be created unless you have thought about it first. I will do my best to provide self-proving examples of how to be responsible and create those things you desire to manifest in your life. If some of the things I say do not apply to you, read them anyway. Sometimes things crawl out from under the carpet that you find do apply to you.

A 'Must Know'
To be yourself as a Soul Being, it is necessary to understand how energy works. Here are two truths that people call lies:

1. **The Law of Attraction works 100% for you.**
2. **Affirmations work 100% for you.**

This energy has been working for you successfully all your life. If the results you receive are opposite to what you expected, then you didn't realise there are two different energies operating here - what you expected and what you actually got.

Why was that?

To find out what you were really doing, I will show you a material example.

Do the following experiment:

1. Fill a glass two thirds full with water.
2. Put a teaspoon full of earth in the glass. Imagine this earth as the rubbish in your Left Mind connected to your problem.
3. When we make affirmations, we have our attention on the experiences we don't want:

We say 'I *don't* want this (bad thing) to happen to me from now on'.

HS doesn't understand the word *don't* (because it is not a constructive word), so does not include it in the sentence. Now the statement becomes an affirmation in its own right and we are actually saying:

'I want this (bad thing) to happen to me from now on'.

Then we carry on and say:

'I want it to be like (this) in the future'.

Unfortunately, the pictures we see of how we want our future to be contains no energy until we actually bring those pictures down to earth and create the necessary action to make them appear as a material reality for us and others to see.

1. We have already asked for the opposite to work for us.
2. Our future can never occupy the same space as now. Only <u>now</u> can occupy present time.
3. As the saying goes, 'Tomorrow never comes'.

Now stir this glass full of rubbish so it looks nice and muddy. When you say an affirmation incorrectly, you are stirring up the bad energies in your mind that are causing the problem, hence the mud in the glass.

Look at it again in about an hour's time. Has the mud gone? No it hasn't, because YOU have done nothing about getting rid of it. All you have done is stated the fact that 'it is there'. So it will continue to be there working against you and causing you the same problem, because that is what you requested.

The reason your negative energy is still with you is that negativity does not exist in the Spirit Realm and your HS understands that what we call negativity is an action we want to improve on, so the negative word (don't) was removed and the affirmation HS actually worked with was: 'I want this bad thing to happen to me from now on'. And it will continue to happen to you because the Law of Attraction and this affirmation is working perfectly for you, 100%.

Now look again at the glass with mud in it. The mud may have settled down, but it's still there, isn't it? To make something go away <u>YOU</u> have to do something to remove it.

You have to create an action to remove it, such as putting the mud back into the Earth where it came from and then cleaning the glass to make sure all the bits have gone. You will know when the action is completed when the cleaned glass make you feel good.

As this is a material example of a mental action, your body does nothing, but you have to remove or change the mental energies that are keeping the memories of this experience with you.

The same procedure applies when you ask for something to appear in your life. 'God please give me £1,000', you say, and hold out your hands waiting for it to arrive. Hang on a minute! When you came to Earth you were never given a slave in Heaven to do your work for you while you sit around watching TV all day. Please get one thing clear - Earth is a DIY planet. If you want something to happen here then you have to Do It Yourself. I must admit though, some, earthbound Egos have learned the art of using people as their slaves extremely well.

In the Spirit Realm it's all about love. Some Spirit Beings will offer you help if that is their mission. No Spirit wants to take your power away and do your work for you. Just ask yourself 'Why did I come to Earth'? You are not here on holiday; you choose to come here to create experiences and to learn from your mistakes. Your desire is to be more like Source. Part of your purpose is to learn how to be a loving Soul, and that's no easy task to perform.

A baby's body relies on others until all its body parts are formed, then it learns how to use them and do things for itself.

When you ask your HS for help, you are offered a few different ways you can create the actions that will make that project a reality for you on Earth. You still have to make up your own mind about which option you are going to try. Nothing is ever done for you on Earth by a Spirit Being. They all know you are a young god on Earth in charge of your own life and learning to be godlike.

Your requests are answered 100% of the time. Maybe you mentally rushed off to someplace else and didn't wait for the reply, or maybe you didn't like the reply you heard. Even the thought of doing something about it yourself may have upset you. Or maybe you never had a clue who you were talking to. Only you know the answer to that.

If you're mentally ranting and raving about not having a slave to do your work, then you have been looking at life from the wrong point of view. Doesn't the truth hurt at times?

SILENT TALKING AND LISTENING

A pain in your body is the only communication you have which tells you something is not flowing correctly in your life. This is the ingenious way Source has created to draw your attention to an incorrect experience you are creating. Pain never appears without a reason. Pain is the sensation you feel when you are flowing mentally or physically in the opposite direction to good. Doing something good never causes pain.

Pressing your finger against a sharp object will cause your finger pain. Banging your head against the wall will cause your head pain. Eating and drinking man-made foods will - over time - cause dis-ease (pain) in your body. Every time we mentally or physically go against a truth it causes some form of resistance somewhere in our body. The cause may be an incorrect belief you are following. If you continue to flow along that direction your body will continue to feel the pain until you eventually feel quite ill. How strong has the pain got to get before we start listen to our body? Pain is the only indication we get that something is not going quite right in our way of living. We love to blame any mental illness on others and any physical illness on to nature. It rained, so I got a cold. No - your negative or unhealthy belief 'I always get a cold when it rains' caused your cold.

You can use a pain to look back on your life.

- **When did you first feel that pain?** How old were you?
- **What were you doing or saying at the time?**

Go deep into that experience and find what you said that formed your negative belief. If you still believe it, then it is still causing a resistance in your body.

- **If you're having trouble remembering the experience, then ask your HS to jog your memory.**

It is important to know, because this information is blocking your progress. That pain may also be preventing you from achieving other things you want to do.

- **You have not let that past experience go**.

If you keep going into your Mind and bringing the energy and pictures of that experience into the NOW then it will continue to cause your body painful feelings. Is your Ego determined that you are right and they are wrong? The pain you are feeling may be telling you something different. Our Ego's survival mechanism doesn't work very well on the subject of arguments.

The false beliefs you're following from the original experience need to be found and corrected, they need to be removed or replaced with a positive belief and then those negative energies will no longer be in your body.

Now you know you are in charge of your life, you can knowingly remove old beliefs. Now that old belief no longer applies to your present day life, then know that you are releasing it from your mind; just let it go, make up your mind never to look for it again. Move on with your life.

EXAMPLE OF A PAST MEMORY

A six-year-old girl was happily skipping down the path singing her favourite song. A dog came out of a house and wanted to join in the fun, so he 'asked' her with a loud bark. The bark frightened the girl, and she fell over and banged her head against a wall, which gave her a headache. The dog thought it had been the cause of the accident and ran off with its tail between its legs.

Everything that happened during those few moments was recorded as a movie by the cells in the girl's body and automatically stored in her Mind. She ran home, looked at the movie again in her mind and told her mum how a dog made her fall over and her head hurt. Mum made it better. The next day she looked at the movie again and told her mates in school what had happened, because she had a bruise on her forehead, and the headache came back or got worse. Every time she looked at that movie to tell someone how she got that bruise, she ended up with a headache.

Ten years later, she saw a dog running down the road with its tail between its legs. That triggered her dog movie again, and she got a headache. She then created a new belief that the fall she'd had when she was six had left her with a weak head, and that was why she keeps getting headaches (false belief). Now many things cause her headaches in life like seeing a dog with its tail between its legs, hearing the song she was singing at the time or any dog barking. She has added many imagined other untrue beliefs to her list of causes. By the time she had reached 20 she hated dogs, got migraine easily, along with other head complaints which left her with head problems. She is still telling everyone how this all started when she fell over at six years old, and that it was the dogs fault. Can you see how the story has been expanded and exaggerated?

The message her HS sent her at the age of six may have been something like 'pay attention when you skip, watch where you are going, don't go into your dream world'. This message she missed or ignored completely. That message is still with her, it is a part of her headache scenario, yet it doesn't apply to her latest headaches. The false beliefs she added later were all added to her dog movie to create her present-day head conditions. This once young lady has created a snowball effect of false beliefs.

She needs to remove the original headache belief from her Mind and the rest will disappear. The rest have lost the reason for being there, so they have become null and void. You will learn later how to do that.

Let's take a look at the energies being directed to Earth right now. They have changed. We have new guidelines coming from the sky. Aquarius is the name given to the new energy hitting earth. One of its energies is to encourage us to look more closely at that personal energy called *love*.

If we continue our old trend of hating and disliking everything, everyone and the body we own, then the cells in our body will continue to give us pain all the way to the grave. We have the ability to kill our body through dis-ease if we are not willing to play the **new game** and show our goodness or 'Godlikeness' to others. If we don't want to play the new game, we have no good reason to remain on this playing field called Earth. So nature works its magic, its own methods to remove us from the playing field.

We have new guidelines to follow and apply.

The new game is called – **Love everyone, including your enemies.**

I don't mean hugging and kissing them. That is not showing your real heartfelt feelings. That method only shows others who are watching how you are supposed to act. That is 100% Ego operating.

First we need to know what the real meaning of love is.

The dis-eases your cells are in will successfully kill your body if you choose to do nothing about this new game. You need to look inside your body and realise you are a perfect 'I AM Doing It All Myself' Soul Being. Nobody can create your life for you.

You need to understand it is the cells in your body that have feeling, not you. Soul beings are the same love energy as Source. How much do you love the creator of your actions - I am talking about your body here?

If you send or *think* hate to or about another person, then that person may not accept your gift. Your hate energy will continue its journey and circle the world. Whilst it is on this journey it may attracts hate feelings from other like-minded people who have their attention on hate (like attracts like is the LoA), it works superbly on negative energy. So your ball of hate now ends up with more hate than it started with, then it thumps you in the back of the neck ten times stronger. It has been lovingly returned, sent back to you as not wanted by the recipient, so your body's cells feel its effect and they are not a bit pleased with the experience **you** just created. Remember, your body creates the physical actions of your choice, but you Soul create the mental actions of your choice.

It is wiser to keep your attention on things you can do that lift your cells feelings to a higher vibration, like creating loving ways to live, which creates better health in your body. Soul Beings love using their energy.

There are many good healing systems on Earth. All healers are doing their best. They do as good a job as their awareness of their subject allows them to. This also depends on how well they understand the energies they are using and what they expect these energies to do in another's body. Do your clients express the benefits they feel during or after a session? Their reply will tell you a lot about you.

Our personal world keeps changing. Earth keeps changing.

Our reality keeps changing. Nothing ever stays the same unless you choose to make your life static.

That means you have chosen not to improve your situation, you have chosen to create resistance instead. Static causes pain in your body's ever-flowing love energy. Can you see how I am getting you to go mental? Can you see how your thoughts kick-start your next creative action?

When Mother Nature does something different from what you want, like pour down with rain when you planned a day out in the sun, you may get annoyed with her because she has upset your game plans. There you go, trying to be a bigger god than Mother Nature. Nature is trying to teach you to become flexible. Are you willing to change your plans?

You need to move beyond the comfort place where you have arrived. You need to improve on many of your experiences. You have done your best to do it on our own and failed miserably.

When your plans have been blocked by nature or others, you need to allow your Higher Self to show you some options you can choose from and, when you choose one to follow, HS will continue to help you to create that experience the best way you can.

It is better to get in touch with, and listen to, the voice from the Right Mind than to listen to the garbage your body's mind is sending you. Do you want a happy life, or a hell of a life?

RELATIONSHIPS

The very first thing you do when your body is born is to create a relationship with your mother. Then you create relationships with Dad, brothers, sisters, aunts and uncles, grandparents. You make friends in school etc etc, so you would imagine you have become quite an expert at creating good relationships by the time you reach adulthood. But you are not an expert. Making friends may not be one of your best abilities.

You have no problem creating enemies with those people you do not wish to be friends with, so what is going wrong here? Why don't you love everyone? The simple answer is, everybody is different. They do things a different way from you and they think differently from you. When you were young some people may have appeared to be quite scary to you.

Nobody ever taught me to rely on my feelings and to accept those feelings that felt reasonably good. Nobody taught me to send feelings of love to others. So I learned to live with others using two downward spiralling energies called 'I don't understand where you're coming from', and 'I am just going to watch you'. I was a quiet kid and rarely spoke to anybody unless they insisted, like teachers in school. So in my junior school I was a loner. I didn't want to make friends or enemies. There was just me. I liked my own company, it gave me time to think and dream.

A change of schools at age 12 helped me to change my 'no friends' rule. I noticed that many of the kids seemed a bit lost with this sudden change of surroundings, so I decided to talk to many boys and girls of my age to see if they had the same interests as me. We formed friendships, joined youth clubs, went everywhere together and had great fun. I accepted them all as they were. I was surprised that everyone had a different lifestyle to me, and this interested me. It was as if I was being forced to ask my friends questions. Sometimes I thought I was being too nosey, but they answered anyway without complaining.

I realise now that asking them questions set my mind at rest. What I didn't know at the time was that asking questions was to be a part of my life purpose. Unknowingly I was testing out my ability to ask questions. Many things we did as a child are connected to the plan we created before we came to Earth. It is as if, over the years, we are gently eased into our reason for being here. Many of the things you loved doing as a child have a strong connection to your life's purpose. All you have to do now is find the pieces in your life that did that.

If you do not know what you are supposed to be doing here, then run through your life and find the bits you enjoyed the most. What were you doing? If you look at your past experiences, you will find they form some kind of picture. They are the early stepping stone that lead you into what you are supposed to be doing now.

Nobody can tell you what your purpose is. That is like asking someone 'What will make me happy'? Only you know the answer to that. You have had enough experiences here to know which of them you really loved and enjoyed doing (don't even think of looking at the bad things). Scan through your life, gradually going back earlier and earlier, and see what you come up with. Also, look at the things you did that your parents told you off for doing. Don't blame them for doing what they did. Parents don't know your purpose for being here. Some can see which way you seem to be heading, but mainly they want you to conform to what they think is the correct way of living.

Any person you allow to control you, including your parents, has been given permission to do that by you when you are in their space and when they are in yours. They are still in your space when you go mentally into your Mind and think about them.

People are acting as your masters if you do whatever they say without question. If you like what they ask you to do then you are being in charge, because you are doing those things willingly. If you dislike doing the things they request or demand of you, then you may feel you are their servant or slave and you complain and protest the best way you can.

Sometimes you are quite happy for them to be your masters and to run your life their way, but you have trouble stopping that game from continuing when you just want to be yourself.

Sometimes when you try to break away, it works out badly and your parents call it teenage revolt. You only want to be yourself and that's not revolting, but being controlled feels horrendous.

You can only create your life in this moment in time known as present time or the NOW. That means there has only ever been one driving force creating your life and that is YOU, the Soul.

Nobody has ever been able to create your actions for you, so you are passing the buck when you do not take responsibility for what you do. If you have been taking the easy way out by following another's instructions without questioning them, then deep down you know they are controlling you. This book is to teach you how to get back into your power again and **Be Your Own Master**. Would you like to take control of your life and be a winner?

That doesn't mean there is no need to follow others' instructions or follow Earth rules. If you are working for someone you still need to follow their formula, but whatever the actual work or actions you create, you do your way to please your Self first. You then know who you really are, and you know you are doing everything your way. This creates a feeling of satisfaction in your body. This satisfaction does not come from the money you receive for doing something; it comes from the pleasure you receive from the actions you create.

You, Soul, are always the **Thinking Being** in charge of your actions, and it doesn't matter what you create. It doesn't matter if you are doing something for yourself or for another. First it must satisfy a desire in you to want to do that thing. If the result pleases others, then that is an added bonus. Your true satisfaction comes from what you create.

In relationship with your body

Life is all about **Energy.** When you go to **the Right Mind**, you Soul are still linked to your body's cells. Your cells feel everything you are discussing with your HS and they show their feeling of approval to the option they prefer to create. It is your body cells that choose which option to create; they tell you through feelings which they feel is best. You also receive feelings from your cells while they create the actions and the feelings they have after completing the actions. If the project did not cause your body any harm or pain, then your body *feels good* about the whole scenario.

When you go into your body's **Mind** and replay or relive a past unpleasant situation, then every cell in your body receives those unpleasant energies again connected to that experience. This is how we bring past pain into present time.

Every cell in your body feels uncomfortable due to the unpleasant energies connected to the past experience you have your **attention** on, and your body **feels rotten** again. You are draining the healthy energy out of your body and replacing it with bad energy from that past experience.

To plan an action you need to:

Be in PT and decide to BE inside your body. You don't have to be in your heart. Be in any part of your body you desire.

Make up your mind what action you want your body to create.

Move into your body's Right Brain, with the intention of moving out the crown of the head to the Right Mind.

Imagine your HS waiting there for your request.

Ask your HS the best way to create the experience you have your attention on, and listen to the options. Your body is also tuned into your HS listening to these options and one of them will make the cells in your body feel quite good. Notice that feeling, and choose to create that option.

Come back into your body and give the instruction to your

body to create that experience. This may involve using physical or verbal energy, or both.

Be there while your body creates the action you desire.

If there are any snags, like things you never thought of at the time, then go back and ask your HS for more instructions. Your body's feelings are always with you.

Whatever you create on Earth involves thinking and teamwork. Living is an inner feeling first, then an outer reality as your body completes the cycles of action on Earth. Others are then able see, or if you are talking, hear, your creation, and pass their opinion about it. Not until your creation arrives on Earth does it become a *Reality*. Now others are able to express their point of view about your creation. Accept their approval and disapproval. You don't have to agree with them, as they see life from a different point of view to you. But you may learn something from their viewpoint. If they disapprove of what you have done, you may learn about something you missed. There is always something to learn. So thank them, and if necessary ask them questions. They are giving you an opportunity to learn from their viewpoint about your creation. Our old way of using energy, 'I'm right and you're wrong', needs to come to an end. Only those with big stubborn egos want it to continue the way it is.

Getting in touch with my HS is a way that works for me. If you have a different Spirit Being you contact and are happy working with, like an Angel or Guardian etc, then use them if you wish instead of HS. There is no reason why you cannot get the same results, as there is no such thing as 'The Only Way'. There is no one stopping you from use the method I use for doing things through your favourite Angel. But please stick to one angel only. Do not ask your questions to your entire angel collection. That's saying you don't trust or believe any of them. They each have a different point of view anyway, so you may get highly confused with too many different points of view.

If it doesn't work using your spirit friend, then I suggest you take a closer look at who you are relying on. Not all spirits are heaven sent; some are earthbound, for reason of their own. Some spirits think Earth is their heaven. An entity may trick you into thinking they are your long-lost dead relation who has come back especially to help you and the family. You will sense their real identity when weird things start happening in your house, like strange noises, unpleasant feelings or smells. If they don't make you feel good, then your body's feelings are telling you to keep away from them. This is your inner tuition talking to you, so stop attracting that entity into your space. If you have a dog, where does your dog go when you call in this entity, or when you sense it is back with you again? Your dog may leave the room as quickly as possible.

This is similar to a group of youngsters playing with a ouija board. They don't know who they are attracting into their space, and they haven't a clue how to get rid of them either. True spirits leave, but earthbound spirits tend to stay around for awhile having fun causing you lots of trouble.

If you do not have anybody working with you in the Spirit Realm, and if what I suggest fits into your reality, then give it a try. Never be afraid to ask your Higher Self questions on what I have said. You will gain a better understand of where I am coming from. I can only offer you reality from my point of view. You have to make up your own mind if what I say is the way you would like it to be for you also. There is no such thing as 'The Only Way'. There are thousands of ways to achieve anything - that's what makes life fun. You just have to find a way that satisfies how you see life. You can even give my way a fair trial before you make up your mind.

If the way you are creating life is causing you problems, then it is necessary for you to change your way and look at life from a different angle, by using a different point of view.

Making your life work is easy. Yet it can be hard and even impossible if you are relying on this world to show you the way. It can't. This world contains the end result of things; it only shows you the things that have already been created. Everything we see on Earth is the end result of someone's creation. New ways come when you use your Right Brain, and get out to the **Right Mind**. This is the place of possibilities where you plan your future. All new ideas come from this place I call 'The Source of all there IS'. There are no black hated spirits up there.

PERSONAL RELATIONSHIP

We have been on Earth quite a while now and we think we know all about relationships, but do we? Some people fall in love following false ideas of love, which I call 'Must Have'. Their love thinks only of themselves. They may rely on a future partner's outer appearance or the job they have and what others think of them. This outlook has nothing to do with true love for the person and what they would love to do for them to keep them happy. The 'between two people for a lifetime' bit seems to be missing.

Each tells little white lies, not to win their mate over, but maybe through *fear* of losing them if they knew the truth. After they achieve their goal of marriage, their true self has no choice but to start showing through in both partners. So all those little things you kept hidden from each other, or didn't think they would ever find out, or be interested in, or thought were not important at the time, or were *afraid* to tell them about, start one by one to come to the surface.

If a relationship is not built on true love and honesty, then it is tolerated for a period of time (called the three-year itch). By then the true nature of each partner has come through strongly enough to break the relationship apart. They often decide to blame each other for the break up. The truth is neither of them had looked closely enough at the other side of the relationship before they formed it. Remember, like attracts like. The Law of Attraction (LOA) works, and seems to show through well on negativity. If your partner is not a bit like you, not a bit on your wavelength mentally or emotionally, then you have little chance of it surviving unless you both love arguing. That may have been the glue that stuck some people together in the first place. Our nature has ways of showing us when we make mistakes.

You never know you have something to learn until you meet resistance along that energy line. The 'Oh dear it's not going the way I planned', is the trigger phrase to start looking deeper into your Mind to find what were your motives in the first place and why you planned it that way. Looking will point out your mistakes not your partners. You should realise that life is not about 'YOU' any more. The game changed the minute you won yourself a partner. The new game is called 'US'.

If in a relationship we neglect to check how our life has changed or is changing and it goes wrong, it may take another three years in another relationship showing similar situations before we realise that maybe we are not as perfect in relationships as we thought we were, or life is not quite the way we expected it to be.

We learn the hard way that games change when we take on responsibilities, it's called 'growing up'. We need to allow the feelings of our partner to be the way they are and accept them as a part of our life (if possible). Relationship problems can be sorted out by getting into communication with your partner with the intention of drawing closer together. Both of you should allow your natural desire of love to show through.

Before embarking on a loving relationship, each should be weighing up the pros and cons and going deep into thought about: Does this person think similarly to the way I want to create life? Can I cope with their quirky ways for the rest of my life? Can I allow them to be themselves and still love them?

If one partner is weak and the other attempts to control them, then one may become a slave to the other instead of a lover. If that is what you both want for the rest of your life then that is fine. There is no correct way to live.

Nobody is perfect; a good partner may smile as they tell you what they feel are your faults. It's normally things that cause them sadness. When that happens it is time for you to find a quiet place, not to sulk, but to chew over what they said; see if there is any truth in what they said by comparing it to your past experiences. Your partner and children can see faults in you which you didn't know existed. We rarely see our own faults, but others see them easily as they are the ones affected by them. We often think we are perfect, and that's fine because it keeps our confidence high, but try not be too egotistical about your perfection. The same applies when we travel the wrong way in life.

Some people knock themselves down by following untrue beliefs they hold about themselves. Their friends may try to prove that what they are saying is not a truth. They may give examples about the good they see in you, but do you listen?

If your partner causes unpleasant feelings to appear in you, then have the courage to talk it out with them. Find the cause. Communication is a wonderful tool.

Your partner may not realise they set these bad feelings in motion in you. When friendly discussions are applied by both partners, your relationship will grow stronger through the knowledge you both gain, not weaker through ignorance. Remember, relationships are created though teamwork, like you with the cells in your body.

The unpleasant reaction we receive from someone after we have created something should encourage us to look inwards first before blasting them with our 'you are wrong!' attitude. Reacting is a common fault. The point I am putting across is: No matter what experience you create, make sure it contains consideration and genuine loving feelings. If the experience you intend to create involves your partner, then get their blessing beforehand, it's much better than receiving their anger or rage afterwards. Communication is a wonderful tool when used properly.

Now that you know you are the master of your own life and that the only energy you possess is love, you can spot and correct any of your non-loving attitude that have happened in your life, and those causing you unhappiness and pain right now.

THE BALANCE OF POWER

Balancing your power from Soul's point of view is like walking along a tightrope. If you lean too far either way, like trying to be too spiritual or being too Ego minded, you unbalance your body and it will fall, and that is a painful experience from your body's point of view. Life is about creating verbal or physical actions with your love attached.

Any body pain is telling you that you have created an experience incorrectly without love attached. Whatever you did or said threw your body's energies off balance. The time a particular pain started, days, weeks, and months ago, tells you when you first created that experience without love. Look at what you did at that time that caused the discomfort. It is telling you how long you have spent getting it wrong, and how long you have been going down the wrong road.

You may wonder why I go into so much detail about pain and not love. Well to keep it simple:

Locating feelings in your body is the only guideline you have to know if you are creating mental, physical or verbal experience lovingly or with an unpleasant emotion attached.

If you are creating with love, your body's cells feel fantastic, so no resistance or pain appears.

When another person sees or hears about your creation and expresses an opposing opinion about it, then a pain may enter your body. Any opposing opinion may rub your energy flow up the wrong way and causes your body pain. It's only their opinion, you don't have to do anything about it, so **let it go.** They are entitled to their opinion. Acknowledge they have said something by thanking them for giving their opinion.

If you do not like their opinion just let it go, otherwise your body may set up an energy called resistance: which say's 'you are right and they are wrong', then your ego comes into play and make another enemy.

If you like being an Earth bound Ego being then *y*ou may start pointing your finger and arguing about who is right, and who is wrong. That's not the best way to live life. Try listening to their opinion and see if you can learn something from it. If there is nothing to learn, then thank them for expressing their views, with a smile on your face, then **Let It Go** - change the subject.

Any energy that flows against the energy you're sending out always causes resistance. Accept their energy as **their point of view**. Resisting causes friction and friction is felt as pain in your body. Allowing the world and others to be the way it is is a wonderful healing technique for your body. Know that you cannot change the world, or other people. Controlling is not a loving action.

You own your body for a lifetime so do your best to love and respect it. It is doing its best to please you. It creates every action you asked it to; even the non-survival actions you asked it to create at times. Remember you are its master; it always follows your commands. You, through your thoughts, are the creator of its health and sickness.

DEFINING THE GAME OF LIFE

Source is the creator of all life and we play the same imaginary game with our bodies. Relying on my imagination makes a lot of sense to me. It brings me closer to the truth. The images I receive supply me with enough knowledge to want to continue playing the game.

I know I am an Infinite Soul. I know I cannot be seen or killed. I know I need a physical body to create my experiences on Earth. My body is the only way others know I am here. They find it difficult to believe they cannot see me, so I don't push the subject. I know they mistake my physical body as being me so I accept and allow that.

On Earth we only see the end product of our creations. My body was my first creation. I'm not asking you to believe this, but where did you get your body from? Isn't it worth following this crazy image system, just to see if it works for you?

WHAT IS THE PURPOSE OF BEING HERE?

The reply to that question didn't come overnight. I didn't really know what I was doing here. The answer kept coming over the year, one bit at a time, in no form of order. Some answers were: to play my games of expressing myself in my own unique creative way; to enjoy myself at all times; and to challenge myself to improve on all that I enjoy doing or saying. It sounds like I was aiming for perfection, even though I know perfection is impossible to achieve in a world full of opposites. So I changed the meaning of 'Perfection' to mean 'Do the best I can' and that made me *feel* much more comfortable.

Some people think they just have to look up into space, or talk to the Universe, and all things will come to them. I tried that method and nothing happened. I couldn't even pretend that something had happened.

At times we have to be really honest with ourselves. I realised it was going to takes a lot more than just wishing or demanding to make something happen in my life. My progress was slow. Sometimes something stared me in the face for about two years before I get the message. Yes many times I felt quite thick and helpless.

I found I could think more clearly when I left the place of chaos (my Left Mind) and got into a place of quiet (the Right Mind), but at that time I didn't know I was travelling from one mind to the other. The awareness of my link to the Right Minds energy never arrived at my doorstep until much later in life.

Let me tell you about my slow progress. It started in 1966. I wanted to know who I was, so I read many books on bizarre subjects. In 1970, I went on a course and learnt that I was a Soul Being. From 1970 to 1985 I knew I was here to help others to improve their lives. From 1988 to now I have been trying to find the shortest way to handle problems, without trying to take short cuts. Short cuts never work; we come up short of the information we need to know.

I studied a way of life that could clear a problem from my body in two hours. Later I studied another system that did the same job in 30 minutes. My question was: if we can install the energy of a problem into our body cells in the space of a few seconds, then why does it take us so long to get rid of this unwanted garbage?

Part of my reasoning was that we have to delve into the chaos of our left brain Mind to find the false beliefs we installed some time in our past. And those beliefs often don't seem to make much sense when we connect them to the problem we are trying to solve right now.

The energies in our Mind are just as chaotic, as the energies of the Source of all there is uses in its mind. That sounds strange doesn't it? Nothing in the mind of 'The Source of all there is' is kept in order. Energy has no form of order, it is just **there**. Order is an Earth word we use to try and assemble our creation in a step-by-step way we can understand.

So as you can see, it seems I am looking for the impossible in the Spirit Realms, yet when I ask for a piece of information from the right mind it arrives like magic. When I reach 120 years old I may have most of the solutions I'm looking for in life, but until then I am quite content to look for the quickest way to clear rubbish from my body by adding more information to the knowledge I already have. Even finding the right question to ask is a problem sometimes, but I refuse to give up.

LET'S RECAP ON WHAT YOU ALREADY KNOW:

■ You know you are the Soul attached to your body.

■ You know you are the only master of your life.

■ You know you need a body so others can hear you and get to know you.

■ You know you need the help of enthusiastic ego to move your body's limbs to create your actions.

■ You know ego creates your body's voice sounds, so others know you are here saying your thing.

■ You know in another's body the only BEING worth talk with and listening to is the Soul, not their ego.

WHAT YOU MAY NOT KNOW IS:

Your body is the only vehicle you have to create experiences with on earth.

Your body is the only transport you have, and it needs to be kept in a healthy condition for the journey, the same way you service your car for a long journey.

Anything you resist creates blocks in your body's energy systems and prevents you from achieving those things you desire.

A misused body may not complete your mission if you shortened its life span.

STRESS IS OUR BODY'S BIGGEST ENERGY BLOCKER

The energy called stress presses against the flow of our life. We limit our unlimited power by saying we are ignorant, not good enough, or just don't know how to do something. We set this negative energy block up and put it into motion for our Self, simply because we didn't know who we were and we don't know we can think for ourselves. We then look for someone whom appears to be cleverer than us, and we follow their way of living. We follow their mission for being here.

Their system opposes our purpose for being here. This makes us feel even more confused, stressed and ignorant of what is going on down here. As we continue on this downward spiral towards oblivion, we use the dark energies that just seemed to be in our body to protect us against everything we dislike about others. We even feel justified to create war against others. Where is the sense in this?

The only thing that really needs changing is the game we are playing right now. This game is upsetting our bodies. We need to get our bodies back on course and start playing the game we came here to play. I'm sure you never came here to make a body just so you could stress it out by protesting about how bad life is here on Earth.

Now that you know who you are, if you don't like the way you are doing something, if it is causing your body pain then it is in your power to stop doing it that way, it is that simple. You need to find another way to create the experiences you enjoy. If others can benefit from what you create, then that's not being full of stress, that's being full of life and joy.

HELP FROM OTHERS

There are many spiritually-minded people out there who live through the love of helping others. They are eager to teach us how to create harmony and balance in our body, and in Earth matters. Rarely do they come to us of their own accord, because that is not the way the game of life is played. When we are ready to learn the master appears.

That LoA truth was set up by Source. We have to put that flow of energy in motion. If we want to know something we have to make the effort to go out and find that someone who knows about the subject we are interested in and talk with them.

Sometimes the answer appears in your head in image format, or on your computer as an email. Your HS loves using computers. A computer's energy works the same way energy works in your body, and in the Spirit Realms. It is wise to listen to, or watch the information, as it is telling you from HS point of view how you could handle the situation you have your attention on.

Even though others help you, you are still your own healing master. You still have to decide if something they have said or done worked for you. You have to ask yourself if this has solved your problem. And your reply may depend upon many Left Mind beliefs you are carrying around and believing.

Most of your beliefs are pure rubbish and belong to others, or they are outdated and belong to your childhood learning experiences. Relying on your Left Mind is a no go area.

It is also impossible for another to know how, or show you how to live your life the way YOU want to live it, unless they are on your wavelength and give you advice you can relate to. Many try and some get very close.

WHEN WE TRY TO HELP OURSELVES WE OFTEN FALL FLAT ON OUR FACES.

We look into our Mind again at those actions we created wrong. We try to see what we actually did or said so we can correct our error, but each time we go into our Mind, there are more negative emotions attached to it than we bargained for, and those negative energies keep motivating us the wrong way. They act like hissing, scratching wild cats in the dark, they distract us and we get angry all over again, and continue to point our finger at others. So your Mind is definitely not the place to solve any of your problems.

I WANTED TO KNOW

I tried pulling my Mind to bits to find the areas it contained.

MY DESIRE AREA:

Here I store all the things I decided to create, but haven't yet done.

None of the actions I planned prior to arriving on Earth are stored in my Mind. That information is stored in the DNA strands of my cells.

When the time is right; when the planets align with my pre-planned purpose, they and my HS filter to me some of the information written in the strands of my DNA so I can experience the next piece of my pre-planned programme.

MY PROBLEM AREA:

Here I store all my unfinished business. These are all my 'I tried to create' experiences I didn't get right, or haven't completed. They are waiting to be corrected or completed at some future time. But my Mind keeps giving me all the reasons why I shouldn't do those things, and backs it up by showing me my past experiences of failure. This area defeats my desire to be perfect in all I do.

MY MEMORY AREA:

I don't have to learn how to do the same thing over and over again like remembering a person's name, because my inner computer stores this information in the DNA of my cells.

MY AUTOMATIC AREA:

Here I store all my simple actions that need little or no thinking. This area causes me problems when I don't think about the reply I am going to give to a person when they say or do something unpleasant in my space. If I don't like what I see or hear, there is a possibility I may automatically 'hit out' verbally or physically in a very unfriendly reactive manner.

MY DOINGNESS AREA:

Here I store all the activities I know how to do. This is the dominant area known as my domain. From here I tend to make myself right and other wrong simply because I know how I do things. I call this area my Ego mind, which is not really a truth, because it is me Soul not taking full responsibility for what I am doing or saying right now.

Wow! In taking a closer look at these different areas where I store different types of energy, I realised where my Mind is. There is a common factor in all these areas. Every cell in my body has strands of DNA which store my experiences as they happen, so every cell in my body acts like a mini Mind recording its understanding of life in its DNA. Each cell before it dies passes its information (and misinformation) on to the cell that is going to replace it. Cells do not think for themselves – they are just recording machines, recording everything that is going on in their space inside and outside the body.

The cells in my feet have a different point of view of the situation from the cells in my eyes. Every cell in my body has its own point of view. But when we put our attention on a past unpleasant experience, every cell in my body chimes in and gives me Soul its personal opinion about it. This is how the movies are formed in my imagination.

I forgot to mention: 'I Soul' also add my thoughts about the experience, which may be true or false depending on my reality of the matter in hand. My beliefs are the icing on the cake. My beliefs are respected by every cell in my body - I am its god. It doesn't matter if my beliefs are true or false; it believes and follows only me.

So I am my own worst enemy. It is my own false beliefs that are rubbing my loving energy up the wrong way and causing my body to feel pain. I have nobody to blame for my physical, mental or emotional ill health other than myself.

My left brain is a telephone exchange that talks to every cell in my body. It also sends out into the world the message of all my cells as a collective. It broadcasts the full movie showing my emotional state for others to receive or pick up on. How many times have you stood near someone and felt their joy or pain? How many times have you tuned into a stranger across the room and instantly liked or disliked them? Proof that this energy exists can be found in Aura Photography. Not only do you have visual proof that they have energy, but you also know what type of energy by the colours they are vibrating at. And some Aura photographers are able to let you know how far your aura projects out into the world.

In my body's mind there is no such thing as true love, there is only a natural animal instinct to mate. My body has great difficulty in accepting that I am love of a different kind.

I want my body to show love from my point of view, but the ego energy inside my body says this goes against its natural animal instinct. It believes in 'Love them and leave them'.

The power of real love removes any confusion between physical and true love. Because of this confusion, we have leaned towards wanting other countries to live our way of living. Hence the 'I'm right and your wrong' attitude comes into play again and causes fighting. So our egotistical earthly way of living has taught us how to fight and separate from each other on a grander scale.

This is why I say: any group that looks at the human body and sets a different value on the male body compared to the female body gained this information from our ancient animal instincts. It has nothing to do with the Source of All Creation.

Unfortunately by using our left brain's animal desires, we bent spiritual truths to suit our ego desires. In truth we are all Soul Beings of equal status. We are all made of pure love energy. We have never received instruction that one half of the human gender is more worthy than the other. We are each blessed with different energies of the whole. We need each other because we each have things to learn from the opposite sex. Men learn how to create actions with feelings, and women learn how to turn their feelings into actions. This balance makes each of us whole.

MY ROLE AS SOUL

I want to create my desires the best way I can.

I would love to create my desires as good as Source.

It is my opinion that some men have closed the door in their Right Brain and have learnt how to use their Mind's imagination to pump up their ego instead, hence the male attitude towards woman and the people of other countries.

It is natural to aim for perfection, even though it is not possible on this dual-polarity planet. Most of us want to be better than we are, so the desire to look at the actions we created wrong is great. We want to look at the actual actions we did or said wrong without getting stimulated again. We want to correct our errors - we don't want to keep blaming others for our faults. We want to know how to create that experience better the next time the situation arises, or correct a mistake we have made. But how do we do that? There is a safe way to delve into the doom and gloom of our Mind without stimulating its angry energies.

BELIEFS

A belief is something we created and accept as a truth that matches the content of our reality of the world. Our reality contains two areas of awareness.

OUR MATERIAL WORLD OF OBJECTS:

We state what we see and others confirm its reality. When we say to another 'I can see a tree', and the other person can also see that tree, we agree that a tree exists. So our beliefs about material objects are **agreed upon realities**. That tends to make Earth appear to be a more solid agreed upon foundation for our life.

We tend to think that this is the only reality we have. But that belief is not a truth, as Earth is nothing but a world of end products. There is nothing on Earth that teaches us how to create. Earth is a world full of things we have already created.

You need to move into another space to view what you desire to create, and view the different ways you can create it.

OUR NON-MATERIAL WORLD CALLED IMAGINATION:

This is an area you probably seldom use to your advantage. When using your imagination you have the ability to make all the experiences you desire to create enjoyable.

When you use your Left Brain's Mind, your imagination **shows you** how bad things were for you in the past.

When you use the Right Mind your imagination **allows you** to see ways to create a good loving experience or how to improve lovingly a past not-so-good experience.

Let's define the energies involved in creating actions a little further.

COURAGE

This is a creative energy of thought which keeps you going along the path you have your attention on, regardless of any blocks you meet on the road. You need to apply this energy to all the positive desires you want to create. Remember you are always going it alone.

THOUGHTS

These are subtle energies that visually show you ways of experiencing, or not experiencing, the thing your attention is latched on.

A BELIEF

This is your opinion about the thoughts you have your

attention on. The contents of your belief attract into your space the energy of thoughts positive and negative.

Example: We believe it to be that way or not that way, according to your reality of life.

Both positive and negative beliefs work for you. Your negative beliefs move in the opposite directions to survival and create pain in your body. HS does not see them as positive or negative beliefs - they are just energies you are asking to come into your life.

Now put your thinking cap on and turn your movie screen on, then read the above three statements again and see if each one is a truth for you by finding and looking at your own examples. This is how we formulate our beliefs to create or not to create actions in our lives. Many of the beliefs you are following, you have not proven to be your truths. They came from other people and may be false. When you accept false truths without proof they can block the purpose you came here for.

Constructive thoughts energise your body. Destructive thoughts deplete your body's energy. You are in full charge of which way you want to travel. It depends on the mental pictures you have your attention on right now. Your body's cells immediately feel the full effect of those thoughts.

On a 0-10 scale: Does 'Work tomorrow morning' making you smile or groan?

If you are continually thinking negatively about something and have been over a period of time, then you have put your body on a downward spiral concerning that matter, and maybe a part or parts of your body are already hurting. If you continue along that line of thought over a period of years, then the death of that body part may be the end result. In a sense if you have decided to stop playing the game of life and stop following the rules completely, you have arrived at a situation of 'Stop the world I want to get off'. And HS obliges you with all your requests so helps you to achieve your latest request. You are 100% in charge of the way your life works or doesn't work here.

A truth is becoming aware of something and accepting it. If reading the above makes you slightly depressed, then what are you mentally creating or not creating that is depressing you? What little thought have you just become aware of?

You may hear or say all the 'I cant's' connected to what you want to do in life. These are the negative beliefs stopping you from moving forward. You may have pains to prove it and you may use those pains as your reason why you can't. We love justifying why we can't do something.

BE GRATEFUL

This is a good time to be grateful for the energies you do have available to you. Your body's energies are the only tools you Soul have to use. Your body is a separate energy unit and needs Earth energies to keep it alive and well, but you are in charge of seeing it receives the energies it needs at the time it needs them, like time to relax, time to eat, time to sleep, time to boost its energies, time to repair its damaged areas etc. This is the way you show your responsibility, respect and gratitude for the work your body has created for you. Remember it has created all your physical and verbal experiences all your life.

TO WORK WITH YOUR HS:

- Go inside your body and into your right brain. Take an almost full belly breath without strain and feel it in your lower belly. As you breathe out, relax all your body's muscles. Continue this breathing a few times until you feel nicely relaxed, or the world has disappeared - it doesn't matter which.

- Now open the imaginary door in the top of your head. If there isn't one there, then put one there.

- Now go out to the Right Mind where your HS is waiting to greet you. I almost forgot: Take with you the 'I can't do' you desire to reverse right now.

- Ask your HS to show you the actions you can do to change this situation into an 'I Can Do'.

- Your HS may show you a few ways to tackle this problem. Choose which way your body feels is good for it to do. Remember this is team work.

- Bring that knowledge to Earth and when you are ready, ask your body to create it.

You have to be in the NOW while your body creates.

Then look at the results. If the end product makes your body feel good, then it's a job well done by the both of you. You couldn't have created that action on Earth without the help of your body.

Actually the energies needed to change that belief were projected into your body at the same time you were viewing them with HS. Every cell in your body was looking at the scenarios with you. As your body is the machine that creates your actions, it told you through feelings the way it would like to create it.

You can put your life back into order any time you wish by following the above simple routine.

Prove to yourself that the belief you just created is **your truth**.

Prove to yourself that your beliefs work for you and that you are always a winner.

Life on Earth is a personal game you are playing, so try your best not to upset others while playing it.

Remember the game they are playing is different to yours.

The trick is to *knowingly* set-up the action in your imagination prior to creating it on Earth.

You are working in two worlds at the same time.

You desire to create a certain thing on Earth. Your cells' energy response helped you to form a belief about that. Remember this is team work. The **Imagined Movie** comes down into your material body before your body create the actions as planned. Soul plus Body achieves your result.

Whatever you prove works for you on Earth builds your confidence, confirms your belief and becomes your truth. You are the creator of your life and your beliefs set the path you take.

When you accept another's beliefs without proving they also work for you, then that person becomes your master and their belief energies send you down roads you know nothing about. You no longer have choices, so their directive energies screw you up mentally, which causes you stress physically. The energies you are trying to use belong to the person who gave you the belief.

You mentally make beliefs now to determine how you intend feel in the future if you create the actions attached to those beliefs. Now is the time to make believe, or make a belief. We should rely on our beliefs when we give our opinion about something. Sometimes we quote another's words as our belief without proving to ourselves that it is our truth as well.

We make believe about things that haven't happened, about non-existent situations. We can make believe in our attempt to create life. Make-believe is a method of solving problems. That type of fun may get us out of trouble.

Make-believe also has its opposite. We find where that place is when we take mind drugs. This takes you on the downward spiral into places where the entities created by your imagination may take you over. It is worse than looking at the movies in your own Mind. Your imagination kids you that everything you are looking at is true. I think they call this place Hell, though I've never been there myself. You never know where you are or where you're going to finish up. They call that tripping when the images control you. Which mental hospital would you like to book into? Be warned, they may try to cut those pictures out of your mind.

We laugh at our children for making beliefs about fairies, yet we are making believe and pretending all the time. Unfortunately we do not treat making beliefs as a serious action, yet it is the only energy that creates our life.

Many of the beliefs we create we attach to meaningless events or to experiences that do not belong to us. We also use them to determine what we don't want to feel hear or see happen in our life. They are opposing belief and they work just as well as our blocking beliefs. When we misuse our imagination we set up our life to look at negative things that haven't happened, or we look at past imagined things we thought happened but hadn't really. As children we all had vivid imaginations. Some of our mental pictures do come from unpleasant childhood experiences, and from other times in our life. By continually dwelling on them we continue to attach more negative beliefs to those events through the years. By continually putting our attention on them, we give these scenarios more power to work against us.

For example:

Let's say I damaged my wrist when I was a kid and it healed and gave me no more pain, so I forgot about it. Then years later I am told about this injury. From that time on, every time my wrist hurts I put my attention on that past experience and wonder if it caused more damage than I know about. By talking about it to others I exaggerated; I formed a new negative belief that I had a weak wrist. I now blame any wristache I get on that past accident. The truth is that my wrist healed and has given me no problem for 20 years.

Whatever we put our attention on we invite its energies into our body. If we think negative thoughts, we attract negative things.

The injury I had when I was a kid had healed. What I actually did afterwards was to feed the new cells in my wrist with some bad information. The cells I have in my wrist now are not the same cells I had there when I was a kid. I fed the genes in my present-day cells with false unhealthy information. My wrist always wants to please me, so it again became unable to do its job properly.

We are responsible for keeping pain in our bodies. We keep the stress of a past unpleasant experience in Present Time by not taking responsibility for what happened; we prefer to point our fingers at an object or a person as the cause of our problem.

We can improve our lives by simply changing old unwanted beliefs. Saying the belief out loud brings the energy out of thought form and into the reality of the material world. It becomes a more solid part of your life. That belief now needs to be reversed.

Your HS makes sure all your beliefs come true - both the positive and the negative ones. HS doesn't understand opposites. Everything is perfect the way it is in Spirit land, so it is up to us to reverse the flow of our negative beliefs with the intention of our life being this new way from now on.

When we got rid of those negative beliefs that say who we think we are, we will still be here living our true identity.

There has to be an 'I' who originated a belief before that belief can exist and that 'I' is who you really are. And that makes you the creator of your life. As you know, you cannot be anything you have created, so you cannot be your beliefs; you are the creator of your beliefs. You are not your body; you are the creator of your body. You are a particle of 'The Source of life' and you are the creator of your life on Earth. You do need the help of that material body you made.

Only YOU can create the games you want to play on Earth.

I will do everything possible to get you to really understand that you are the Soul attached to that body. I am not doing this to please myself but to please you, when you realise that only YOU as a Soul Being can change anything in your life. No other part of YOU is capable of doing that, because your body gets lost in the fog of your Mind's past unpleasant emotions.

You cannot remove any of your personal beliefs, as they help to create your personality. But you can reverse them and make the opposite come true.

You have to believe that you can create your life from your beliefs. Therefore I am creating my life from my beliefs.

You can change your life by reversing, revising or removing any belief you find to be blocking you from moving forward, and by removing any outdated or untrue beliefs.

FOUR METHODS WE USE TO KNOW SOMETHING

1. **Mentally:** We understand it. We blend it into our reality level.
2. **Physically:** We experience the knowledge by getting our body to create the necessary actions. Our body feels the effects of what it is creating as pleasure or some form of discomfort.
3. **Emotionally:** The cells in our body attach good or bad emotions to the actions created, depending on the stress or joy the muscles feel while creating it.
4. **Recalling a past experience:** The cells in our body relive the experience and feel all the emotions attached to it.

The first two ways I use all the time.

1. I put my attention on something using my imagination. I create the movie using my imagination, then make up my mind if I want to create that experience on Earth or not.
2. Earlier I created the mental side of that which I now have my attention on. I get my body to find the tools needed, and physically create the actions so I can see the end product.

This is the best way of learning more about your creation. Now you have materialised it others can see it and express their opinion about it. That's a good learning curve, and that's what Earth life is all about.

You are the <u>cause</u> and the <u>effect</u> of your creations.

If you are not impressed with the feelings others attached to your creation, then look again at what you did and find what set those feelings up in others, or yourself.

1. You can correct any physical or verbal part you didn't perform very well that made you or others feel bad.
2. You can gain more knowledge and improve your awareness by creating that experience a different way so it makes everyone feel good.

You can also be the effect of situations you do not create by keeping your attention on it. Taking your attention off it and allowing the world to be the way it is will remove any experience and feeling that do not apply to your life. By doing this you remain the creator of your life, not the effect of the world. This keeps you at ease over all that happens to your body while in present time.

When you created a body to experience Earth life with, in a profound way you became the creator of many possibilities.

When you practise being who you really are, it is much easier to separate your Self from the effect of whatever experience is upsetting you. If you are looking at something unpleasant you can create a distance between the disturbing actions going on, or the thoughts and feelings you are having, by physically walking away from the area and observing the situation from a different place.

Mentally when you Soul quieten your body down and move into your Right Brain, those disturbing energies are no longer in your space, or a part of your life. When you do this switch, you gain peace and freedom from the outside world, from your immediate situation and from your body's Mind traps.

As a Soul being you can change any of your creations you dislike by changing the negative beliefs that are attached to that creation. After that you must energize your body and put that new changed belief into action. It only takes seconds to do.

The 'who am I really?' process you just learned enables you to distinguish yourself as the creator of your experiences. Now you know who you really are, you are able to put into practice the art of reshaping your creations by physically or mentally creating them again to suit your new reality level.

So your next creation on that subject will be different. You will see the end product of your changed beliefs. Your new positive thoughts, feelings, and behaviour on that subject will naturally not contain those old negative energies that caused you the problem. Your problem vanishes when you use your new state of awareness. You learn how to create better actions, which makes you feel more perfect.

To 'Lift your Spirit' and feel good about your Self, it is worth taking a closer look at your role in playing the game of life.

SOUL TRAVEL

First you need to look more closely at one of your abilities.

Every Soul has the ability to travel in the **Land of No Time**, and we all do this often when we sleep or daydream. We have always space-travelled. Peter Pan is not the only one who can fly. Anyone who spends time thinking about another person goes as Soul to where they feel that person is now, or was when they saw them last. When you put your attention on a problem you travel as a Soul Being to the place where it was created. You often relive past scenarios while trying to solve a problem. Sometimes when we go in to our body's Mind area we just point a finger at the person we feel caused the problem, but that depends on how angry we are. Solving and blaming are two different energies; one heals the situation and the other drains our body's energy.

Sometimes we arrive at a time when we have more problems than we can handle; we end up with more problems than answers. Then we may get the feeling we cannot think straight, or cannot do anything right. These are the negative energies in our Mind getting the better of us. When we reach that point we are what I call splattered all over the Universe, which is a truth from your body's point of view. You Soul are flitting from one problem to another without solving any of them.

Hey - I thought we were talking about Soul Travel! What has the body got to do with that?

When you want to be with your HS for a while it is wise to follow a set procedure. Go to a quiet room, chuck the cat out, turn your phone, TV and radio off. Slip into something casual that doesn't cause any tight feelings to your body. Now take a deep belly breath and as you breathe out, deliberately relax every muscle in your body.

Ego may think it's night time - nothing happens at night other than your body topping up with Earth energy ready for tomorrow's activities. So you trick ego into going to sleep while you keep your attention on relaxing your body's muscles.

If you find other thoughts are still with you, then your attention never left a recent problem. Make up your mind to let the world go, and put your full attention on what you are doing right now, otherwise this relaxation will not work. Remember you are in charge and you cannot be in two places at the same time.

To deliberately relax the body to a point where the world may disappear for awhile, you need to go into your right brain, then breathe in deeply from the base of your belly area to the count of five. This brings more oxygen into your body than chest breathing. As you breathe out to the count of five, mentally tell every muscle in your body to relax, and feel them doing that. Each time you breathe out you want your body's muscles to relax even more. Your body loves doing what you ask it to do. When it feels completely relaxed, just enjoy the quiet and let your body do its own healing for awhile, which you need know nothing about.

When your body feels relaxed this is a good time for You

Soul to leave your Right Brain and go out through the top of your head to the Right Mind. I call this place in space the Spirit Realm.

You have to create these actions every time you go there. Nothing will happen if you put it on automatic.

Now imagine making contact with your HS, who is always there, and mentally give your HS a problem you would like to solve. No physical words are needed - just use your thoughts.

Intuitively listen to the reply. Your inner tuition may offer you a few ways of solving that issue. You may think you are making it all up, but that is impossible. You wouldn't be asking the question if you already knew the answer.

So what comes through is the answer. Ask as many 'How do I do that's' as you like to the answer you didn't fully understand. You want to know exactly how to solve this problem.

The cells in your body are listening in to this conversation, so as they are going to create the actions let them choose the way they can do it the best. Now quietly pop back into your body. You now know without doubt how you intend to handle that situation with love in it, and your body agrees with you. Don't forget to thank your HS for its assistance.

When coming back into your body, don't be a crazy driver and come screeching back in - if you do you may bounce around inside from your bum to the top of your head a few times before you come to a stop, just as a new-born baby does before it learns how to use its brakes, and that may be a little uncomfortable for your body, so always BE a good driver, drive safely and stay in control. Have you ever seen the shudder a baby makes when it wakes up sometimes? Bad driving, but it soon gets the hang of it.

Rocketing back into your body is not a new experience for you. When your body relaxes as a precaution it ups its sensitivity 100 fold, so it is alert to any dangers from the outside world. A pin dropped may sound like a gong being hit.

When you are drifting off to sleep during the day and your phone rings, or your waistband or some other garment feels much tighter than you thought it was, or some strange noise happens in your space, it disturbs your body, so you Soul come back like a rocket to find out what is going on. Your body's early warning system just went off - it's working perfectly.

That's why you need to turn off your phone TV, radio and chuck any animal out of the room before you start meditating. All those Earth things can be distracting and prevent you from completing the mission with your HS.

UNINTENTIONAL SOUL TRAVELLING

Your body needs your help. It's always waiting for your next instruction to do anything, or to solve a problem, but you have gone walkabout! Or is it fly-about, I'm not sure.

As a 'Soul Being' you're flying around all over the place looking at all your problems, trying to handle all of them at the same time. Life doesn't work that way. You cannot solve problems by going to the places that caused them. There are too many negative stimulating energies there. You need to go to the quiet place where your Higher Self is, and work with one problem at a time.

Life is all about how you use the energies available to you while here on Earth. On Earth your life experience is seen by others in different ways. You get your body to create material objects so others can see your masterpieces. You reshape the appearance of your physical body with smiles and frowns so others can see the emotion (Energy motion) you are feeling and using right now. Others can see if you are happy or unhappy while creating an experience.

You also construct some of your masterpieces verbally, so others hear your words of wisdom complete with your emotions.

We continue creating our life experiences all our lives. There are no times when we are not doing this. It becomes quite a habit. We do it until we decide to stop playing the game of life with our body. We then complete the last cycle of action with our body. We created its start. We change its action all through our life. Our last action with our body is to stop the breath of life entering it. Then we go home. We are Eternal Beings. You should gain comfort from knowing we never die.

Looking at life from eternal time, we come to Earth to gain knowledge, to gain understanding, to improve on our awareness of life and to enjoy a short holiday with other Souls.

SAFETY PRECAUTION

No matter how many times you escape from your physical body, there are always energy links attached to it. One of the most important energies attach is called **Responsibility**.

Also attached to your actions, thoughts, and words is the

energy called **Loyalty,** which also forms your link to the Right Mind. You were loyal in the beginning. You report back the way you experience earth so Source knows what living on Earth is like for you. HS is also attached to that energy line. HS always knows what you are up to, yet it never interferes or judges you.

These two links cannot be broken by you; Source built them into your body's computer system. It's like the two-way link a mother has with her baby. It doesn't matter how old that baby gets or where it goes in the world, the love link is always there, even if you kid your Self you dislike them, or they dislike you for some reason. That link is always there, working its magic in both directions. Your child will always be a part of you. It doesn't matter if you are their mum or dad.

The energy link that goes out of your **Right Brain** to the Spirit Realm and HS is 100% under your control. You have the ability, and the right, to turn it on or off as you choose. You can talk or not talk to your HS as you please. You are in charge. But you have no control over the incoming information from Source and your HS. At times when it pleases you, you may show a deaf ear to what is being said. Just as kids do to their parents at times.

So let's get back to Soul travelling. The cells of your body record everything, including you're 'Out of Body' trips. Every cell in your body records everything you do from its point of view, as well as what is going on inside and outside the body at that time. If you the Soul have been travelling too fast, and going to too many places all at once, your cells get confused and frustrated. They cannot keep up with you, your attention is not on one thing long enough before you're off to the next location. Remember: the energies in your body move at a much slower pace, so it gets very concerned when there is too much movement. There is a limit to how much movement your cells can cope with. Some people cannot cope with the change of motion certain fairground rides create. Their speed and erratic motion disorientate them, which makes some cells in the head feel dizzy, and the cells in their stomach feel sick.

When you Soul sense a distress signal coming from your body, you know it is time to go back inside your body and check out what is causing the problem. You shoot back in and look for what caused it. 'Too much movement' was the reply. This is why you need grounding at times. You need to make sure you are fully back on Earth, in the body and in full charge of it again.

You as Soul cannot be in two places at the same time, so these two exercises are to get you out of wherever you are and bring you back into your body.

EXERCISE IN SIMPLE GROUNDING

Grounding has nothing to do with digging a hole for your feet to go in. A plane when landed is grounded and can still be moved from place to place. Grounded, for a plane, means its wheels are on the ground.

Your universe is your body. When you come back to your body you are grounded. You can still move your body from place to place. You are grounded because you are here on earth, back in your body.

Sometimes when you come back you are not grounded, your thoughts and attention are still elsewhere, so you are not really back in your body.

To be here you can only see those objects that are in your

space right now. So look around your space and recognise a few objects. This will bring you right back into Present Time.

AN EXERCISE THAT HELPS YOU TO FEEL RELAXED IN YOUR BODY

Make a mental note of how your body is feeling right now. Mentally move slowly through your body and notice any tension, tight muscles or feelings of discomfort.

Breathe in, filling your belly with oxygen. On each out-breath, think the word 'relax' into a tight muscle until the tension relaxes.

If you sense any dark energy in a discomfort area, then on your out-breath, breathe out the discomfort from your body until it disappears. Continue belly breathing until your body feels relaxed and comfortable.

FEELINGS ARE SUBTLE ENERGIES

Become aware of what your body is telling you right now. Is it hungry, tired, full of energy, lacking energy, annoyed or pleased about something? Through your body you get to know how well you are living your life.

If your attention is constantly on worldly matters, then you may not be taking care of your own body. There is nothing you can do about the outside world, so allow it to be the way it is and accept it. This prevents you from loading your body with distressing thoughts and energies that make it feel sad or weak unnecessarily.

People's loving feelings easily get turned off, and their negative energies switch on when they involve themselves in situations that have nothing to do with them personally. If they have no intention of taking action by offering help, then there is nothing they can to do about the situation. Just allow the world to be the way it is. Otherwise you are being unkind to your body. Half the news we read and see on TV pulls our body down and makes us feel sad, which may be good for the drug companies, but not for your health.

EGO'S ACTIONS

To convert your imaginings and thoughts into words, ego relies on a program which makes the voice box in your throat talk. You Soul do not have the ability to creating anything of a physical nature, so you have to rely on Ego to dig out the computer program which interprets your thoughts so the right words come out of its mouth. It only says what you want it to say; it has never been given the ability to speak for itself. Only cells have the ability to speak for themselves by sending out their feeling energies.

This is why we should show our ego some respect. It always does a very good job. You should treat ego as your friend - why make an enemy out of the only physical action creator you have? Ego is at its happiest when it is getting the body to create the actions you desire. You are ego's master - when you are in your body, that is. Ego cannot do or say anything off its own back. Ego doesn't have a brain of its own and it doesn't have a voice.

We often blame ego for things we actually told it to say or do. This happens when we as Soul look into our body's mind to find how to make our life work. That mind is full of how we reacted to life in the past. It's full of unpleasant emotions that have nothing to do with how to make our animal body become human. If you want to know how to make life work and be in harmony with others, then you need to go in to your Right Brain and out of the door in the top of your head which takes you to the Right Mind.

Only when you are in your Right Brain can you connect with the Right Mind. Only in the Right Mind can you talk with your HS and discuss how to create a more loving, human way to handle situations. Source is the Right Mind.

There never has been and never will be an energy called love or harmony in your body's Mind. Its purpose is to store all your mistakes and all your failures so you can correct them at a later date. In that mind there are some beautiful harsh words and very strongly barbed emotions. If used well it can successfully show you how to create enemies by using actions and words that oppose being human with love and companionship.

Most of us have been taught to rely on our body's mind to create our reality on Earth. Just take a good look at the outside world and sense the mental results we are creating between groups of people. Does Earth feel like a heavenly place to you or does it feel quite hellish?

Keep out of that mind if you want to move forward, but stay in it if you want to continue on the downward spiral and live life backwards - which spells _evil_.

WHAT WE CAN DO TO GET OUT OF THIS MESS

The first thing is to know that you really are in control of your body. So be in charge and relax it out of its 'stressed out' feeling. You want to get your body back to doing its proper job of keeping it self-healed and living in harmony with others as soon as possible. This can be done by going back into your body. Go into your Right Brain, then quieten your body down by meditating for a few minutes, then talk to your HS about what you intend to do next. You learn how to create your experiences better when discussing them with your HS.

Maybe the state we are in at this moment makes it impossible to make our life work, especially if we are not tuning into and listening to our body's feelings. Some of us are not tuned into our belly's feelings when it says 'I'm full'. We need to change that habit of not listening to the body's feeling. We also need to be in touch with another sense known as our sixth. Our sixth sense is the one that has the ability to get us out of any mess we are in.

YOUR SIXTH SENSE

Now you know you are the Soul in charge of your body, you have the ability to communicate with it by using an energy known by your body as the SIXTH SENSE. You Soul **are** the sixth sense. That is the same energy Source uses to talk to you, but Source calls it **Love.** Source created a universe using this energy. And you lovingly created a universe, known as your body, by using your sixth sense. You lovingly created your body, yet knew it really belongs to Earth. This was your first Earth creation. You also know your body relies on your love and instruction, and on Earth energies to make it work.

EMOTIONS

Every Earth energy is energy in **motion** and has two ways of moving according to your desire:

- You can make it move forward by lovingly flowing with the energy of life. This helps your body to survive.
  Or
- You can misuse this energy and move it in the opposite direction, which causes friction in your body. Your body feels the pain of any physical or mental actions you care to create. Pain drains energy from your body.

MIS-EMOTION

Miss-emotion means using energy the wrong way round; like using it for a non-loving non-survival purpose to weaken or destroy another in some physical or mental way. When we are being mis-emotional we are using the wrong energy for the experience we are having. Why cry at a wedding? Why laugh at someone when they hurt themselves? It weakens our body's energy, pulling us down to a non-survival level of existence.

As a pure Soul, **Love** is the only energy you have to use. The pineal gland in the head interprets all energy your body receives into a reality it can understand.

Unfortunately you have sick cells in our body that are still attached to some past experience that didn't go right for them - that's why they are sick. They don't know how to get out of that past experience, they are still angry about it. Their miss-emotion distorts your love by showing you a reverse way of living in the world.

We also use our love when viewing energies we put our attention on that are not visible to our body's eyes. We call it using our **imagination.** Again, if we use our imagination while in our body's mind, it may produce energies that are not loving or creative but lean more to being destructive to others.

IMAGINATION

You may find this to be a better description of the word 'Imagination'. You use this energy to form what seems like invisible picture of possibilities. You use **imagination** to communicate with your HS, your Angels and to any Earth person who is not in your space but in your thoughts.

Words are the vibrating energies your body's ears pick up. You cannot see words, yet your ears and body cells feel the vibration of their energy. It is wise to learn how to use our sixth sense and tune into the Right Mind to live a better way of life.

If what I have explained up to now seems real to you, then keep reading, there is more fun to come.

The energy unit I call the **source of all there is** appears, according to the way I look at life, to have gone walkabout.

Some people visualise Source in a human form, but that is not possible. To me, the body of Source IS the Universe we see in the sky. Source has created its own body of energy, yet we cannot see Source. And nobody can see you, the Soul Being, in human form. Your personal universe is your body. It is through your body that your energy can be felt but not seen. So know when you look up into the sky that you will only see the body of Source. And when people look at you, they only see the body you created and mistake that for you.

Everything Source has created is stored in its mind. This is where your HS goes to retrieve the information you ask for.

Although Source cannot appear to you in physical form, you are able to sense and feel its love in everything it has created on Earth. The Spiritual name I call Source is - **'I AM'.**

The same system applies to your physical body. You cannot appear in a physical form to your cells, yet they know and feel you are the **'I AM'** presence, in every thought you send them.

The galaxies in the body of Source are similar to the organs and other energy systems in your human body. They are all linked together and play their part in forming the pulsing energy called **'Life Force'.** Each small piece of the picture fits into a larger piece that gives us more awareness, which fits into a larger piece that gives us more awareness. You Soul are a small part of Source living on a molecule called Earth which is also a part of Source that gives you more awareness.

That indicates to me that we are an important part of the system, but we don't know a lot yet because we all have great trouble controlling the universe called our physical body, and we all have great problems in keeping the ground we play our games on clean and free from rubbish.

We are at the stage of learning, where we love making a mess, just like all kids do. But we haven't learnt what the word mess means yet.

ARE YOU READY TO GROW UP?

The planet Pluto has changed its teaching energy. It has stopped teaching us how to fight like babies with each other and is now directing us into our teenage years. In Earth terms this is where boys and girls realise they are different. New energies are arriving in our body that may be causing us some embarrassment, similar to the embarrassment teenagers go through. I have noticed more people of all ages are becoming forgetful. It may be connected to the amount of rubbish that needs to be removed from our minds.

To give you a better idea about this mind rubbish: when a bomb explodes its outer case shatters into millions of pieces called shrapnel. It remains on Earth as unwanted rubbish.

Pluto has just completed our last learning curve of how not to live; it sent us into War with the World for a second time. Enough is enough. What did we learn from that lesson? We thought there must be a better way to live; those A-bombs nearly killed the lot of us.

Now let's move over to our children. When we see our children doing something we don't like, we shout at them. Wow! A mental bomb just went off in their mind. We never ask them – what are you doing? Why are you doing that? They were happily trying to work something out for themselves, but we didn't ask them those questions, we sent them a mental bomb that exploded in their mind and all that energy shrapnel left messages in their mind – I'm not good enough – I can't do anything right – I'm no good etc, etc. Everyone has mental shrapnel in their mind, and being forgetful may be Pluto removing some of our shrapnel.

Sometimes when we watch a child trying to do something, we know what they are trying to do and we help them to achieve it. When we *think,* we don't always get it wrong.

Let's take a look at the teenagers of both sexes. Unknown energies quietly tell them that they are different and have a special role to play in the game of life. This involves meeting up, getting to know each other and playing the relationship game. They take the first step by learning how to communicate with each other, with the intention of seeing if they are in harmony with them. At this stage we don't realise we are looking for this special someone.

Pluto is now sending all of us similar energies of learning how to live in harmony with each other. This episode of forgetting things has arrived to rid us of our past ways of living with each other and with the people of the world?

Pluto's time of breaking up relationships is now over. That was easy to learn, that was kids' stuff, anybody can do that. Now, are you ready and mature enough to learn a new game of how to create love with others? Are you willing to do your best to keep your personal relationships together at all costs? That's real new stuff for us kids to learn. So are you ready to grow up and act like a maturing teenager? Remember teenagers learn how to live in the company of each other, yet still make mistakes. It is not possible at this time to ask your parents how to correct your relationship errors. You may notice most parents haven't yet learned the art themselves.

We have a long way to go before we as the human species reach the stage of adults in our maturity - just look at the way we treat others in the world. In some cases their skin is not the right colour, or their features are not the right shape. We still have a lot to learn about being human. Killing humans only temporarily removes them from Earth. They all come back with more knowledge of how to fight another day, it was part of our game of life.

PLUTO'S ENERGIES

It was around 1988 that the new Pluto energies started trickling down to Earth. It affected our awareness, which in turn affected our present-day consciousness, which made us feel a bit uncomfortable. This energy gently forced us to come out of the 'I don't want to know box' we have been living our life from.

Health shows and psychic fairs started appearing everywhere. People became more adventurous and came out from behind closed doors. They were slowly opening themselves up; they were curious about the real truth about their existence.

Later UFOs, crop circles and orbs appeared in greater numbers, and for some reason our old electrical equipment started failing, yet we were not afraid. Our awareness was being changed. This helped us to realised we are not the only beings in the Universe. Pluto's energies are gradually increasing in strength. They are now affecting our bodies as individuals. Lots of mental stuff has started happening, like sleepless nights, dreams of past experiences, forgetfulness, unusual aches and pains and many other weird and wonderful things, all happening to lots of people at the same time.

I got the impression that the energies we automatically

saved are no longer needed; they are being churned up and removed from our memory banks. Out of courtesy at times we are shown the items they are working on, hence we may feel unusual pains and strange upsets. The reason for this was way beyond my awareness level until I had a chat with my HS. Then removing those energies was no longer a mystery to me.

Pluto is preparing all **'I AM'** Soul Beings so that they can eventually tune in to the other dimension, known as 'the Spirit realm', without being held back by their Minds reactive blocking energies. This will make it possible for Souls who have forgotten how to travel to travel without fear.

Your body will remain on Earth as usual and it will greatly benefit health wise from your walkabout experiences. Pluto may soon become very, dare I say it, energetic, in bringing our physical body cells into line with our new way to live. The DNA in your cells is being altered as confirmed by the writings in the crop circles we were recently shown. We react rather strangely to crop circles; we are more interested in who created them than in the message they are sending us. We do the same with spirit beings who contact us. We are more interested in the name of who is talking to us (for bragging purposes) than in the message they are giving us.

The energy of Pluto is also creating changes in our weather and causing floods, fires, hurricanes and freeze-ups beyond the normal for the seasons, as well as earthquakes, all larger and more powerful than normal. When do the fireworks begin with volcanic displays? Whoops, they're happening already in Iceland. Maybe Source is using this time to dig over Earth's garden ready for a replant. My goodness, haven't we left a mess!

The most important character in the Spirit Realm for you is you're HS. In a way you can say that HS acts like the heart of your physical existence. Your HS gets the information you request from the Source of all there IS, so you can use this energy to live life in a more heartfelt and loving way.

Source and HS are in constant communication - via email or cell phone, whichever, who knows.

Source has created its energy body perfectly. Earth is part of the body of Source, and your material body is a scaled-down version of the Universe we see in the night sky - or is it?

The Universe in the sky may be one cell of the body of Source. That means there may be millions of universes up there that stretch way beyond our imagination can accept or cope with.

You tailored your existence and chose your place of birth, which complies with the experiences you intend to create this lifetime. The only little problem you have right now is **you have forgotten who you are and why you came here**. You have no choice but to get things wrong if you do not have a clue about what you are supposed to be doing here. That's common sense, isn't it?

The cells in your body are doing their best to tell you, but you are still getting things wrong, as indicated by the discomfort your body feels.

Should you ignore your body's warning signs, your cells start giving up. They are actually saying; 'If you're not willing to play the game you came here to play, if you don't want to listen to us cells, then you don't need this body any more'.

On Earth, if you have no intention of playing the game you

are playing by the rules, then you get kicked off the pitch and maybe off the team. In the Spirit Realm, if you do not intend to play the game of creating your chosen experiences, then there is no need for you to be on Earth. So you may get kicked off Earth's stage, you could say by choice.

Now that we have successfully screwed up most things on Earth, Earth now acts like a cancerous cell in the body of Source. Maybe that bad cell in its body brought Source's attention to Earth's plight? Maybe our physical body is not the only place where we create cancerous cells because we do not fully understand what we are doing.

As Source heals, Earth heals, and so do its occupants. But there is a little snag here, because you are 100% in charge of your body and your life on Earth. You have to be willing to make the changes needed in your life. Nobody can do it for you, so which way do you really want to travel?

ALL CHANGE - WE HAVE BEEN TRAVELLING IN THE WRONG DIRECTION

We often do things the wrong way round by accident, because we didn't know any better at the time. Sometimes we learn quickly, depending on how painful the experience was. Sometimes it's too late, because we have already told someone about the stupid thing we did, or someone saw what we did. Some people prefer to laugh at us instead of helping us, which adds weight to our pain.

When our attention is fixed on creating an action, we seldom pay any attention to the effect it may have on others.

We are only interested in what we intend to do, without considering if it would upset others. When we look at life from a point of view that says 'all about my Self only', then we are living backwards. How do you feel about the other Souls in your space? Do you ever put any of those feelings into practice?

WE ALL NEED TO START HEADING IN THE RIGHT DIRECTION.

You need to reconnect your end of the link to your HS, so you can get the correct information you need to make your life work the way you want it to while staying in harmony with your body and with others.

There are set procedures for you to follow when creating experiences on Earth. There are easy ways and hard ways of doing everything. Throughout your lifetime you have learnt the hard ways, and had many failures in the process. Now you can learn a more pleasant way of creating your life experiences.

But you need to follow a different set of rules to live a balanced Earth/Soul life. Sorry, my mistake, they are not rules - they are guidelines. It's so easy to forget which world I am working from. Rules are controlling, and needed for Earth living due to the effects opposite energies create including gravity. No desires to control you ever comes from the Spirit Realm. Instead you are offered guidelines that keep you in charge of your body's life.

Your HS relies on the 'Book of Knowledge' that Source gave us, also known as 'The Source of All There Is'. HS finds the information you ask for from this book and offers solutions for you to browse through. Remember you are being shown a few of the possible ways to accomplish your task. You are shown ways that match your awareness and your reality level. There is nothing definite in Spirit Realm. It is up to you to choose which way you prefer to perform the action to achieve the results you desire.

In Spirit Realm you are not controlled by anyone. The experience you create on Earth will be more enjoyable when you learn how to listen, how to see, and how to understand the options offered by your HS. This makes it much easier for your body to choose a way that *feels* best for it to accomplish.

PITFALLS IN THE AFTERLIFE

Oh dear! I believe that not all Souls move directly into the light after they are finished with their body. Two observations caused me to come to this conclusion:

1. The feelings a dog and I felt during the war, from a presence we sensed in a cupboard under the stairs of a bombed house. I was about eight years old at the time. The hairs on the back of the dog's neck stood on end at the time I felt this presence. It was obvious this soul hadn't left Earth.

2. Why are gargoyles on church roofs pointing out, and some downwards? They are not there to scare the birds or parishioners away. They must be there to keep those out of the church who may not know they are dead. Yet I would have thought they were the souls who needed the most help.

If a Spirit tries to communicate with you, it may be one of your familiar angels, and if it sounds as if it is trying to control you in some way then know it is most probably an Earthbound Soul. That Soul has never left Earth's atmosphere. It may not even know it has released from its human body and it may be trying to carrying on with its normal Earth life. Not all earthbound Souls are gentle. Their energies can be quite vicious and destructive, as found by youngsters who play around with oui-ja boards for a giggle. Is this why they put gargoyles on church roofs?

Gargoyles prove that imagination is real, and as powerful as earth's emotional energies. Some earthbound souls stay here, trying to prove a point, such as why they should not have been executed, or treated in such a disgusting way. They are what we call in limbo, in a time warp. Actually they are in a no time zone. Without a body, time does not exist for souls. Some souls well past their sell-by date are just wandering around wondering why humans won't talk to them. They haven't realised that their body has died, they still mock it up.

Nobody has said all Souls go to a god-like place when we leave our body for good, have they? We still have our power of choice.

When using our bodies on Earth when we have completed an action like cooking a meal or digging the garden, we clean the tools we used, ready for the next time we need them. The same applies when we leave our bodies permanently. We are in a place or situation where Earth's opposing energies cannot affect us.

Most Souls show some respect to the body they used. They

stay around to make sure it is disposed of respectfully before going home. It's like showing respect and thanking it for the journey it took them on to gain knowledge and awareness.

Some souls, when looking back on their lives, realise they never created anything right and they panic. There are many reasons why they are afraid to go home, so they stay on Earth, maybe hoping to correct their errors, or they may think Earth is a heavenly place anyway, who knows.

Do we really know where our HS gets all its information from? I assume it's always from the 'Book of Knowledge' that Source wrote. But on very rare occasions some other Spirit insists they pass their information directly to me. Perhaps they are a specialist in the subject I am following. I don't really know, or is it that I have completely forgotten how the Spirit Realms works? That sounds more like me.

I made a big mistake one day and asked a spirit for their name. The vibrations I got back from that question were not very pleasant. 'My message is of interest to you, not who I AM'. That immediately put me in my place. Now I can't brag to others about who my helper was. I learned fast from that lesson.

You can see why I prefer to rely only on my HS for information and why I allow my HS to act as the doorkeeper of my personal club called My Universe. My HS puts its protective glow of light around my body and only allows those wise Spirits whose glow is equal to or brighter than mine to pass their knowledge to me on the subject I have my attention on. Only those spirits can talk to me personally. Most times they pass their message to my HS, who relays the information to me.

In reality our path through Earth life is not really a lonely one. We just need to learn how to tune in again. Going it alone has never worked for you, has it? Even if your ego thinks it has.

We would have to show a lot of respect to energies we know nothing about if we were allowed to visit the Spirit Realm. It would be like being on Earth allowing a little child to amble around a busy machine factory, where welding sparks are flying everywhere and moving parts keep shooting out all over the place, swinging arms keep zooming over their head. That child, through lack of knowledge, could easily get injured by the motion of all that energy if it was on its own. But that child could be shown around by a guide and taken to safe areas to see how things worked, and only allowed to see those things it could understand.

We are never chucked in the deep end of any experience. We do that ourselves when we rely on the rubbish we have stored in our body's Mind. The same applies when you try to go to the Spirit Realm. You are never left to explore the Spirit Realm on your own, that would be much too dangerous for kids like us.

The Spirit Realm is full of energies that are way beyond our understanding. We have enough trouble trying to learn about the energies that exist in our animal body. That is why your HS always gets the information you need for you.

You will always be invited into the spiritual cinema where you can visually see the different ways to create your desire. It is called the room of *imagination.*

Each movie shows a different way to create the experience you desire to have on Earth. There is more fun in creating lovingly than in rushing through life and creating without a road map.

I hope this information is helping you to gain some

understanding of the way I see souls, spirits and energies working. I can assure you, you are not here on your own. You are not here to be controlled by Earth Beings, or by spirits trapped on Earth.

SOUL WORK

If you don't know the rules of the game you are playing here on Earth, then I doubt if you are playing the game correctly. We have forgotten the rules of playing the game of life. We are not playing the game properly when we maim, kill, or upset the energies in our body, or in the bodies of others.

We have not been given the right to control others. That is not part of our game. We are little baby Souls learning how to apply the first rule of survival in human bodies.

Up till now we have learnt how not to survive as a human species, and that is good. That should have encourage us to act like *thinking beings,* and to start looking in the opposite direction to see how we can survive on earth.

But our mentality may not have reached that great height yet. We need Pluto's energies to showing us how we can do this.

If you have a desire to be different and want to know a better way to live life, then ask your HS these questions:-

- What can I do to get out of this mess I'm in?
- What do I need to know to change my way of living?

In chapter 1 I explain how you are really the Soul occupying your body. I said you had the ability to put your attention on anything and visualise it, and your body has the ability to see those images as well. Your body tells you exactly what it is looking at. This whole process is called team work.

Now is the time to put this process into practice and see if you can make it a part of your reality. You need to prove to yourself that this is also your truth. Knowledge is useless information until you apply it. So do these exercises and you won't get left behind or confused when applying your abilities.

EXERCISE

We will start with an easy exercise, and then move to an easier one later. See how your mind plays tricks with you. I bet you were 'thinking' I was going to say 'something more difficult later'. It takes that long for your beliefs to take control over you.

Exercise using your **imagination:**

Sit comfortably, close your eyes, take a deep belly breath through your nose and as you breathe out through the mouth, relax every muscle in your body. Do this breathing a few times until you know your body is completely relaxed with no tension anywhere. Check your neck and shoulder area.

Keep your eyes closed, and mentally put your attention on an object you know is in the room. (No peeking).

Mentally inspect it by looking at it from all angles.

Keep your eyes closed and describe what you are looking at in as much detail as possible, then open your eyes.

If you really understood chapter one, then who looked at that object? Yes, you, the Soul Being. You put your attention on something with your body's eyes closed, and you asked your body to say what you saw. That's teamwork.

This is real simple stuff we are dealing with here.

Accept the fact that you are the Soul in that body, not because I said so, but because you just proved it to yourself. Knowing you are the Soul in control of your body, you no longer need to hold onto negative beliefs when you find they are not your truths.

What if the voice in your head is telling you 'it is difficult to drop an old belief I have carried around all my life'? Now you know you are in charge, you can reverse the above Belief: That's just your mind talking to you again. Now you know you Soul are in charge of your body, say 'I can change any belief I find in my body that is blocking me from moving forward'. Then tell your mind 'I will change that belief right now. It is easy for me to change any belief I find that is blocking me from moving forward in life.' There, I've done it.

That only took a few seconds to do, but make sure you believe your new belief using the energy of **determination**, so it is not **just words** coming out of your mouth.

Any time a belief pops up in your head, take a good look at it and discover if it is true or false. If false, immediately remove it by reversing its contents. The LoA works both ways. It is so easy to do. Simply reversing it causes its energy to flow the other way, from negative to positive, and the pain it was causing stops.

MORE ABOUT BELIEFS

All your beliefs affect your body's energy system. Beliefs are used to create, or not create, your actions, and they also form your personality. Sometimes when applying a belief your body may end up with less energy, so if this happens it is wise to find the sneaky belief that is causing this down feeling, and if it belongs to someone else remove it from your body. But if it belongs to you, then replace it with an uplifting positive belief related to that subject matter, so it creates a good feeling in your body. Then your body's energy will rise.

You will know when you have found the right uplifting belief when the cells in your body put a smile on their faces and on your face too. You may feel excited with the new idea, or you may feel empowered with its good energy with your body ready to move forward along those lines. You Soul should always consult with your body's feeling before doing anything. Remember it's team work: You cannot do anything without the help of your body, even talk.

Only through the feelings your cells give you can you get to know how well you are progressing with your creation. Every movement your body makes is a creation set in motion by you, unless you're playing at being a zombie.

Some people just rely on their heart feelings. Their ego thinks the heart is a special piece of equipment that does things for them. Well, life doesn't work that way, I'm afraid. Your heart does nothing for you, it can't. It doesn't have a mind of its own and it is programmed to only do things for your body. Your heart is a part of your body's computer programme that pumps your energy around it. It does not think for itself, so it cannot do anything you ask. Because we didn't know who we were, some people nominated their heart as being them. Well that was a good idea to believe in, but not a truth. Well done for trying though.

Only you Soul have the ability to create actions using your body. No parts of your body can be your slave and do things for you. There is nothing on earth that can or will do the work you Soul came here to do. Sorry, you do not have any slaves in your body.

You have learned the bottom rung of the ladder. Only you can get your body to create actions that experience life the way you want it to be.

It will be impossible for you to move up the ladder of life if this fact is not a truth for you: **'My body is preventing me from experiencing life'**. That is a 100% false belief.

The true belief is **'You are doing things to your body that are preventing it from creating your actions'**.

Only I tell my body what to do – That should be your understanding and your belief. If that is not your belief, then your next step will seem unreal, and the steps after that will become more confusing or impossible. Then you will fall back into your being-controlled game again.

We all live our lives in the direction our beliefs take us. Our beliefs are created from our thoughts.

If you desire to move up the ladder of creating new experiences, if you have a desire to improve your creative ability in any areas of your life, then you need to look for any negative beliefs you have that are preventing you from gaining the knowledge needed on that subject. They need reversing before you can gain that knowledge.

It doesn't matter what you do in this world, you always have to start at the bottom and make that bottom step real first.

1. That first step is formed from the thoughts that energise your imagination. Your imagination changes your thoughts into picture format ideas. You need to be well away from your body's mind to do this. You don't want blocking tactics coming in before you get started, so relax your body and go into the right brain, then out to your HS. This brings you into your imagery planning room, where you and your HS talk things over and work out the details of how best to create the action. The cells in your body are listening in. Remember your body creates the actions for you, so you need to listen to what your cells have to say. Your cells' decision is always the correct way to create.

   It's like washing the dishes. When you were young you had to learn the washing-up procedure. You had to start with a sink and put the dishes in it. You cannot start by drying the dishes first. That only dirties the tea towel, and that wasn't part of the plan. There are some young people who think that's a quicker way to wash dishes, but they never planned on the clump round the ear they got from mum, or the angry words they heard for washing them that way.

   I know that example may sound stupid, but that's the way life is. We do things how we want to first and learn afterwards from our mistakes. Also we often try to take short cuts by starting something halfway up the ladder. I still have many things to learn from my own screwed-up actions. I backtrack to find what steps I missed, what I did wrong, or didn't do. It's so easily done when you Soul have dropped out of the here and now and gone to someplace else. When you are not here paying attention to what your body is doing, that's when things go wrong.

I daydreamed a lot when I was a child and my favourite trick when making coffee was to put hot water into a brown cup - it didn't taste a bit like coffee. That was, and still is at times, my favourite trick. I'm sure you have your own favourite 'oh dear I've done it again'.

Some people get so serious about living; they completely miss the funny side of it. The joke is on you. (Body talk) Err!! Hot water in a brown cup is not funny when you taste it.

Don't get annoyed, just laugh at yourself, and accept the fact and allow yourself to be a big idiot at times. I own top place, my ego says so.

Life starts by getting to know your Self. That means knowing and believing that YOU ARE the SOUL in charge of that human-shaped body you created. Now this has been brought back into your awareness (many times) we can press on to step 2. I didn't want you to ever forget it.

You are doing step 1 when you are thinking about something, then you made your mind up about how you would like to create the experience right now.

NOW YOU GET INTO TEAM WORK WITH: YOU – YOUR HIGH SELF – AND YOUR BODY'S CELLS

2. Contact your HS and ask (in thought form) for the best way to create this experience. Your body cells are listening in. They are used to being a part of this energy trio. You will receive from your HS possible ways to create that experience. You only receive information connected to this desire.

   If information starts arriving about other things, then you have dropped out of your right brain and gone into your body's mind.

   You have to learn to be in control. I know all this is new for you, so go back into your Right Brain and start again.

   Listen to what your body cells are feeling concerning each option offered by your HS, then let your body cells choose the way that makes them feel happy. Remember your cells are the creators of your experience, so they want to be sure they do not cause any harm to the body in the process. Those happy feelings which you feel indicate they have found a way. Should you ask your HS other questions on this subject, they will be answered.

   You MUST stay in THE NOW, and in your body while having this imaginary conversation with your HS.

   By following this procedure you will be aware of any pain your body feels when viewing the options. Your body chooses the way it would like to create it. The best way has no physical pains attached.

3. Now you have to bring that imagined information down to Earth and make it '*real*' for others to see or hear. Your body always creates it in the place of your choice.

   Basically you just have to BE HERE and watch while your

body creates that experience. That is the real meaning of **Being Here** and **Being Grounded.**

Just BE here in this moment in time; in the NOW, directing your body to do each piece of the scenario in its correct order. If that is a new experience for you? Good isn't it?

Your life up to now has been a big rush to do something or be somewhere, or somebody, automatically going into your Left Mind and following the wrong information. You had forgotten your link to HS, you had forgotten who you are and you were never reminded when you were in school. What a disgusting way to live life. You were taught to be a puppet.

HS' connection to you has always been open; it's just that you never listen to it. You most probably thought that the voice you heard in your head was just another weirdo and mistook it for normal ego chatter.

We never phone HS to find the best way to do things. From an Earth reality point of view it's madness trying to talk to someone who isn't there, isn't it? I mean, we are so far gone from the truth, we think there is only this material world worth bothering about. No wonder we get upset when others knock us down. There has never ever been anyone around to pick up the pieces, and help us get out of this mess and back on track. If we told somebody about the depressed state we're in, we would most probably be rushed to hospital with a label on our wrist. And they may try to remove that memory from our brain by using whichever method they see fit to cut it out. They wouldn't dream of look for the emotional energy causing the problem and removing that in a verbal way. That may take a lot of time. And time costs money. Wow! Who is following what god here?

EARTH'S ENERGIES

Source created Earth's energies opposite to its own on purpose. We call half of these energies negative, as they appear to obstruct our body rather painfully from achieving those things we desire. From a spirit point of view, we call them 'dark energies' because they oppose our Light energy called Love.

Light can penetrate and brighten our dark times. Yet darkness dims our love light. From an Earth point of view our body needs Earth energy to create actions. It takes three energies to make our body work properly. Remember your body is an earth object.

1. Earth energy's are needed by all the cells that make up our muscles and by all the other cells that operate our computerised systems in our body. Earth energies enter via our mouths in the form of oxygen and food, and via the perineum at the base of the body. Earth energy is the positive end of our body's electrical circuit. It keeps our animal body alive.

2. The Spirit realm is the light unformed energy of our body's circuit. We have not invented a word that explains the nebulous unformed energies that are swirling around in space. We use them prior to creating our actions on Earth. From this (light unformed) energy we transform darkness into light. When we stop supplying our body with our light of love, it dies naturally.

3. You Soul are the 3rd energy. You supply your body with Love. This is the only energy you have to offer it.

Also when we look at the stored dark experiences in our minds, they dull not only our senses, but our light as a Soul being. Earth's dark energy makes less of us. So your body need all three types of energy for it to survive.

THE INS AND OUTS OF LIFE: NATURE GUIDES OUR FEELINGS

There are three places we can be.

Nature adds an unknown energy to our life. We are always in control of our body, but we need to keep a check on the weather conditions. Earth's Nature is a programme set up by Source which constantly changes. It randomises our life to prevent us from getting too set in our ways. We depend on the weather conditions to either change our plans, not to go out if it is too severe, or we go out and learn to cope with the conditions. The same applies to the energies in your mind.

Now you know who you are, you can **go in** to the rough weather conditions (energies) of your mind, and do battle with those energies, or you can **get out** of your mind any time you wish.

You can **go in** to your right brain, then **go out** to the Right Mind and have a pleasant chat with your HS about something that's bothering you. Then **go in** peacefully to your body and go about your business with this extra knowledge.

Earth has been created so that we Souls can experience life

whichever way we choose. Earth is your playground and nature sets your background.

Children do not have the mentality to understand the above system, so all children need a playground where they learn how to do things for themselves first, then with other children later on. They learn how to create things by using their body and being the effect of Earth's energies. When in school, children also learn how to make friends and play with each other.

As each one of us is a part of Source, we are all here learning how to be the Source of our own lives. So what better way can we learn that lesson than by looking at the painful mistakes we make? They are just dark energies stored in our Mind. Sometimes we pretend they do not exist, but trying to hide from them doesn't work. That approach has never solved any of our problems. Dark energies never make us feel good. They rub our life energy up the wrong way until the body feels pain. We would like to feel good and loving all the time, but that will only happen after we learn to correct our errors. So put your attention on a personal experience that doesn't make you feel good. Now you need to choose which way you want to go with this upset.

Choice 1: You can continue to blame another for your mistakes, which causes your dark energies to attack certain cells in your body more strongly.

You may add more dark energies to that experience by including negative thoughts, feelings and beliefs you are creating right now about that situation. You are making things worse for your body and it will get physically sicker if you continue to follow that route.

Choice 2: Deep down inside you know what you wanted to do or say but may not have known how to do it or say it correctly. You need to look again at the experience and find if any of your beliefs caused you to create it that way. If yes, then find out if that belief is really yours or belongs to another.

Remember love is your true identity, so remove or reverse any bad beliefs until you are ready to come up with a better way to create that experience.

You know that correcting your errors without pointing your finger at yourself or others is the best thing to do. You know you want to feel good about creating this action, not lousy. Your jumbled thoughts and confused feelings only cause pain to the cells in your body. Also, you can always talk to your HS to find the best way to solve this situation.

In all our actions we always do the best we can using the knowledge we have at the time. Sometimes while creating an experience a new way flashes across the mind. That flash came from your HS. Other times we know and feel how bad an experience we are creating. That may come from one of your past experiences, or may be your HS is trying to jog your memory that doing it that way will not work for you.

When these times happen, your HS is actually talking to you and saying you are creating it incorrectly, have you thought of creating it this way? Always listen to what is going on inside your right brain.

It is natural for Earth to pull you down when things go wrong, leaving you with bad feelings. That's the way we learn here.

Take a look at a time you went to the park, or to the beach, and it rained all day. How did that make you feel? All your plans were washed away and you may have been pointing your finger saying 'Mother Nature was controlling me'. Actually that is not a truth.

If you predicted that the weather was going to be fine and you were wrong, then you hadn't taken into account that Mother Nature has its own reasons for creating the weather the way it is. Only when you oppose something the way it is does it feel you are being controlled. You can always **accept** what is happening to be the way it is and change your mind about the activity you are going to do now that it's raining. You can still come out the winner if you are prepared to **allow** what is happening to be the way it is. Just change your mind about the activity you're going to do and you will be happy again.

If you were in Present Time, if you were in the NOW, living every moment as it happens, then you could use your thinking ability and 'imagine' some other activity to do that is under cover. So you can always be in charge. You don't have to allow rain to spoil your day. Simply think up some other place you can go to create something else that makes you feel good. Remember you are a thinking being.

Unfortunately we are so used to following our set procedures that we forget that nature follows its own set of rules. It is up to us to bend a little and **allow.** The energies of Nature are much more powerful than us and we need to learn to accept that and change our plans so our life continues to flow in a pleasant way. But we can only do this when we are in the here and NOW, in this moment of time.

Do your energies feel unbalanced? Then who or what is controlling your thoughts right now?

From a mental point of view, find what energy is invading

your space and choose to do something about it. Don't let it take you over. If a past experience is making you feel sad, know that only your mind contains these unhappy thoughts and images. That experience is not in your present time life right now, so get out of your mind and do something positive about those pictures, or your mind will drive you crazy.

THE REALITY OF LIFE FROM AN ENERGY VIEWPOINT

Living on Earth can become confusing if we don't know and understand this information.

LOVE IS NOT AN ENERGY.

Everything starts from a particle called love.

LOVE just IS.

Love is Source, which released Love particles of its self called **Spirits**. Some of these Spirits create particles of Love called **Souls**. Soul, when in the correct mind, project Love into its actions.

Energies that oppose love have been installed on earth by Source which helps You Soul to create your games; mission; and reason for being here with love.

You Soul attract into your body other particles called neutrons and protons. These particles, working as a team, have the ability to create images we call pictures, and these pictures turn into movies.

If you **Soul** have your attention on something, pictures start forming in your head and you may think they are real.

Everything you see on Earth is made up of assembled particles of protons and neutrons that we call **Matter**.

Mental Matter is **Energy** held together in **Space** and kept together by your body in picture form using **Time.** We call this our memories. This is also the way material objects persist on Earth and this is why your body's eyes can only see those parts of the material world your attention is on in the space you are in.

As Soul you have the ability to assemble particles into shapes in your mental space that your body recognise. We call that using your **imagination**. We love creating new movies, either true or make-believe. With make-believe we pretend they are real.

CONSTRUCTIVE IMAGINATION

Soul is a creator of material, which uses body and earth energies to materialise its desires so others may also reap a reward from your creation.

Your ability to create comes from your ability to tune into the 'Right Mind' via your body's **Right Brain**. This is the area where we form those actions we want to create on Earth. At this imaginative stage our creation does not contain Earth time. Our images disappear as soon as we take our attention away from them.

First we assemble a possible experience using the **imagination**. We use the body to go out to the right mind, then the body's cells are also linked to the right mind, our cells understanding every detail we mentally create. This allows the body to work out the way it wants to create the actions. It depends on your body's desire to create those actions and the amount of energy it has.

When you have worked out what you intend to do, you

bring that *Imagined Movie* down to earth and the cells in your body create the masterpiece for you.

Earth time comes into the equation as your cells store this movie as part of your life's creation. Then the movie persists in the cells of your body as memory.

Your body's cells can only view that movie when you Soul put your **Intention** on it. That movie is held in your mind and becomes energised each time you do that.

Your body will create that experience again when you Soul desire it to be created. It is now fully under your command. This is how we materialise our **Dreams** and create our reality.

The actions your body creates are stored as **your experiences.** Each experience is stored in your past as you continue living the next moment in time.

This present moment last forever. Its energy always flows in the **Now**. Now is the only space you have to assemble ideas in the Spirit Realm and create verbal and physical actions on Earth.

We often choose to take on board the energies of other people's beliefs and accept them as our own without proof. They are not our energies and do not connect to our purpose for being here, and they may causes problems to your body.

When you put your **Attention** on a past experience you bring its energies into the Now.

WORKING AS SOUL TO CREATE THE PHYSICAL

If you want to draw a sketch or diagram, you go into the Right Mind and create a mental picture of it first. Then you bring down to Earth a copy of what you imagined so your body's hand can draws it using pencil and paper according to your instructions.

VERBALLY

If you want to say something, you create a mental picture of what you intend to say; then bring it down to Earth so your body's throat cells utter those words through the mouth.

Everything you do or say is first created in the Right Mind's imagination room. Then you transport it to your body to physically create it. You use your body to materialise all your beliefs and desires so others can see hear and feel your creation. That is the game we play on Earth called living in a body.

Should you hold the belief that **- Only things in the material world are real or true -** then you are missing out on 99% of the real knowledge of living. If you only believe in the end product of your creations, then you are oblivious of who you really are and how you create it on Earth in the first place. You are back in the old game of pointing fingers at others for your mistakes.

THE RIGHT MIND

This place is in the Spirit Realm, wherever that is. This is the place where you talk to your HS and plan your future. This is the place where you assemble the movie for your next creation.

If you have planned nothing for tomorrow, then that is what you will create tomorrow. When you plan nothing new for tomorrow then you will be the effect of the world, and may relive yesterday's automatic actions and yesterday's boring habit patterns again. In addition you will be the effect of any new energies nature and others care to throw at you. You are not creating your desires, so you are not in charge of your life.

FUTURE LIVES

There is an ego-created fallacy about the future that needs to be looked at more closely and brought in line with the Truth. The fallacy is that – **we have lived future lives.** Some people think we can look at things we have done in lives we have yet to live.

The Spirit Realm is where the nebulous book of **All There Is** exists. This book contains all possible possibilities as already created, tried and tested eons ago by Source its self.

These people who feel they were looking at the future were most probably shown by their HS something they need to create in this life that looks futuristic to them. Source has not created a book called **all that will be.** We cannot blow a candle out before we light it. The scenario they saw was a figment, a wish, a desire of their imagination of how they would like life to be in the future. All they need to do now is find out how they can make their life that way, then create that way on Earth and it is done.

Or it may be something they mocked up earlier and have not materialised on Earth yet as promised. Only they know why they are looking at that scenario. If what they saw surprised them, they may jump off the subject in amazement and quickly create a new belief for themselves in panic. They may have seen another civilisation living in another universe, or in another part of our universe. In the Spirit Realm there are only possibilities. Nothing is solid or tangible.

In Earth terms, we cannot arrive at a future time. If that was possible, then you could see yourself on the other side of the road coming back from the pub before you got there. If so, you have just missed a drink.

The truth is, the flow of eternal life moves in one direction only towards our future. We can look back and view our past. We can start creating the material part of our future in the Now. You need to understand and accept that energy only flows one way.

A child pretending to be a fireman or a nurse relies on picture books or recent life experiences to create its mental actions. It is definitely not living out some future life experience. The imagined experience it is living now may encourage that child to become a fireman in the future, if it happens to be connected to its purpose for being here.

If you want something to be solid, then you have to bring it to Earth and make that image solid by materialising it. You have to create it, you have to put it there yourself, verbally or physically. All material objects are the end product of someone's past thoughts. There is no such thing as a future NOW. Our future consists of possibilities only. Past memories continue to exist because we are able to recall our past experiences and invite them back in to our present moment space in picture format.

When you look at our life energy it flows one way towards infinite future. Life energy cannot run backwards when we apply other energies that come from the Earth. If we apply them the wrong way round, which means without using our love, it upsets the forward motion of our life and becomes painful to the body.

Your body doesn't like anything that attempts to reverse its energy flow. It's too painful. This proves life cannot have its direction reversed.

Only Egoistical Earth Beings create reasons why they insist our nature must follow their way of thinking only.

Pain and sadness felt in your body is you Soul somehow blocking your natural flow of energy.

We can reverse most things on earth, but we do not have the ability to reverse Nature's Natural Laws created by Source.

At times Earth's energies appear to be more powerful than those of Source, but they aren't. It is just we Souls digging our heels in and trying to move deeper in the wrong direction. We think we are advancing. We think these Earth energies will support and lead us into a wonderful future, but they haven't up to now, and they won't in the future. Not even on our dual-polarity planet can we make energy flow backwards. All we can do successfully is to painfully block our own natural forward-flowing motion.

I am not saying advanced beings do not come to Earth. They have come in the past on missions to teach us things we need to know at the time. Maybe Mozart, Einstein and others are intelligent beings who came here to raise our vibrations.

That doesn't mean they came from the future; they just happen to come from a more advanced civilisation than ours. People who have really lived a future life should have a much higher intelligence than the rest of us if evolution means anything. If that was a truth then they would be able to solve many of our problems. If they can't, then why are they here? If anything, they might realise how stupid they are to come to a life that is much worse than the one they came from. Who wants to go back to hell, or be a cave man again?

So where do brilliant people get their information from?

Mozart was playing the piano at an early age, and not a teacher in sight. He was composing music for an orchestra. He must have found some way to see an Earth orchestra before he put that mission in motion.

I wonder if they have televisions in the spirit realm. He knew every instrument he wanted to use and how he wanted them to sound. Did Mozart come here on a mission to lift the spirits of the human race? Could it be that when he arrived on Earth he spoke to his Higher Self, who directed him to the music of the Universe so he could create his masterpieces?

So I'm sorry folks, you haven't had a future life. Only in the now can we create things for our future and we have to live that now. You are 100% in charge of creating your life, and no Spirit being will take that responsibility away from you.

All your life on Earth you can create Images and plan on how you intend to live in the future. You set the first steps of that dream in motion now and build each step to completion before you look at and move on to the next step.

Know the way it works. Your future is the way you plan it in your *Imagination*. Now you can create it that way. If you change your mind and no longer wish to create what you have already planned then that's fine, there is nothing or nobody stopping you from creating something else instead. If you stop creating altogether, if you don't give your body something to do, then it thinks you have no further use of it and starts to die.

This is a natural phenomenon for all unused objects. If you don't use your car it rusts and rots. If you don't live in your house for a while, rot and mildew may appear. It is not only your body that needs your presence. Your energy enhances the life of many material things.

FORTUNE TELLING

There are many ways we can be reminded of our purpose for being here. There are people who have the ability to read hands, cards and crystal balls, which show us our future possibilities. I used to believe that predictions are not definite happenings. Over the years I changed that belief.

Over 50 years ago, I was with somebody who was interested in having their fortune told. We were both invited into the booth and I reluctantly had a crystal ball reading followed by having my hands read. Three of the predictions have come true. I remembered each prediction after the event had happened. No dates were given, except that the last prediction was for something that would happen when I am old. I am still working on the subject this last prediction foretold. I know it will materialise.

I find it strange the way my interest moved off the subject for a while, yet I was drawn back into the subject the reader mentioned. I did not want the last prediction to come true. I refused to follow that path for about eight years, yet unknown to me it was ticking away in my background. My employment was ended abruptly, in the space of three minutes. I faltered afterwards for a few years, and then slowly got back on track. Deep down I knew that last prediction was to be fulfilled, even though I didn't want to believe it or follow it. In Spirit Realm energies flow forward and by following your feelings they guide you to the next stepping stone of the purpose you set up prior to arrival. I have since learned how to stop resisting and to allow. Now I am willing to accept and welcome what will be. I feel the last prediction may happen after this book is out.

BEING GROUNDED

This means being HERE, in Present Time, and saying to yourself; *'I know I am here in my body on Earth right now'*.

This was not an easy lesson for me to learn. All my life only one foot touched the ground occasionally. I have never been quite here (take that which way you like), but really, every time I put a foot on Earth, I used it to hop off to some other place I had my attention on. When I was young, my mum used to say I was always dreaming. That wasn't a truth to me. I was just looking at things that were in a different place to where my body was.

Being grounded means coming back to Earth, in charge of your body, ready to create your next experience with it. This is the only space you have to create your experiences. As you create an experience, it automatically moves out of the NOW and into your past.

NOW IS THE SHORTEST SPACE OF TIME
THAT LASTS FOREVER.

I doubt if you will find a more truthful contradiction. Yet we have the ability to be in Earth time and connected to the Spirit Realm at the same time.

This is because the senses in your body are connected to you Soul all your body's life. Even when you leave your body to space travel, your body's feelings are still with you. It is your body that tells you if you have arrived in a good or bad place according to the movies and beliefs you are storing in its cells.

A RIGHT MIND – DEMONSTRATION

Let me prove to you the reality of space travelling by introducing you to the Right Mind:

Remember you are the Soul; a unit of pure love energy.

You rely on your body's feelings at all times, no matter where you travel to.

Close your eyes and keep them closed. You have no use for your body's eyes in this exercise. You are going to use your ability to see as a Soul Being.

1. Take a deep belly breath, and as you breathe out relax all the muscles in your body.
2. Continue gently deep belly breathing for a while, and feel all your body's muscles relaxing even more on each out breath. You are 100% in charge of your body's state and actions.

3. When you put your attention on your Right Brain: You have arrived in that space. You always ARE where your attention IS. You can BE no place else.

4. Imagine a glass ball in your hand. Feel the texture of its surface. Does it feel smooth, warm, cold? How heavy is it?

5. Now change its surface to frosted glass and see how that feels in your hands.

6. Now change it into a spiky ball. How does that feel?

7. Now open your eyes. Thank you.

What happened here is you went into the Right Brain and created the images I suggested. You inspected each image and your body made up its mind if it liked it or not. Your body created an opinion, and you formed a belief about it. You did this three times in all. You Soul created three different beliefs.

Did you notice the quietness? There was no mind chatter going on. That only happens when you go to your left brain's Mind.

You have also stored a memory of that experience. The proof of that is: you can mentally see those three balls again any time you wish, can't you? You don't have to create them again. They are already there in your mind's memory banks. Those glass balls have become a part of your history.

Can you see now how easy it is to store rubbish in your Mind? You have no use for those glass balls whatsoever, but they are stuck fast in your Mind. They are not offensive, so they will cause you no problems.

If at some future date you see glass balls, like on a

Christmas tree, or watch somebody playing with glass balls, it may remind you of the glass balls you created. There were no other energies attached to this creation, so this little movie will never upset the cells in your body. Only when your opinions contain non-loving energies do your beliefs cause your body problems.

WHAT IS A COGNITION?

It is when you become aware of something. It's having a realisation about the mental pictures you are looking at. It's when you know you have arrived at a truth. It's when you have the answer to something. Cognitions make you *feel* good. Some people say it's when we have a brain wave.

When the energy of this knowledge arrived in your Right Brain, every cell in your body values that piece of information. If they like the idea, they make your body smile. Now you know where your 'good feelings' come from. They also come from true statements you say, like: 'It's a good day' or 'everything is going well', according to your opinion, and you are always right in your own universe.

BAD FEELINGS

If on the other hand you do not wholeheartedly believe what you are hearing, seeing or saying, or if your statement is non-loving, then the cells in your body always speak their truth. They make your face twist into a frown, or an angry scowl. It may make gestures with its arms etc. The cells in your body never lie. Your body's feelings link the reality between your imagined world with our material world.

WHERE DO FEELINGS COME FROM?

They are the energy vibrations your cells transmit when sensing something they like or dislike in their space.

The good side always causes our body to feel joy and enthusiasm. So let's take a look at the bad side of something.

Let's say some information has arrived in your space which upset a group of cells in your body. This causes those cells to feel unhappy. They feel the pain, so others see your body with a miserable face.

Your body is not happy about the verbal energy its ears are hearing or the energy you are mentally creating right now.

You may have forgotten you and your body always work as a team, so you are now feeding your body bad energy. All unpleasant *emotions* (energy in motion) go against your flow of love causing friction in your body. It causes the creative life-giving energy in our body to slow down, stop, or run backwards. This causes friction, and friction *always* causes pain or discomfort in some area of our body. All the cells in your body know about this upset, yet it doesn't affect all areas the same way. Though all the cells know about it and may feel a little low, most can cope and still smile through it. When you're feeling a little low, your body is saying 'something has happened that has upset me'. Your body does not have its full amount of life-giving energy, or it cannot use all its energy because 'that experience' has drained a part of my energy and slowed me down.

Negative or dark energy drains the light power stored in your body. And the source of that light is you Soul. Your low body energy will cause more problems if this non-survival subject is dwelled upon for a long period of time and if not corrected by you and brought back into alignment with your loving nature.

Learn to tune into your body's feeling at the time you are thinking these bad thought, or while reflecting on a bad past experience. You should be there realising this is not the way you want your life to be, so find and correct the error of your mental or physical actions.

When your body is not at ease, know that you have created using your imagination, emotions, or some physical action that your body is not at ease about. We call this dis-ease, which we recognise as a named disease in our body.

DIS-EASE

A dis-ease is a feeling that something is not flowing correctly in our body. We like to add names to our condition according to which area of our body we feel the pain.

All this started from an **unpleasant feeling**, or **sensation,** caused by an unhealthy thought or by something we imagined was not correct according to our way of seeing life. Our belief could be wrong.

CONDITIONS

Nothing gets healed by handling a **Condition.** A condition is the end result of a **Cause**. The energy of a cause is being applied, which creates an effect. There is always something causing a condition, and it is the cause that needs to be looked at and worked with to get rid of its effect.

If you are outside and an icy wind is making your body feel cold, then maybe the wind is the cause of that condition. If you go indoors and warm yourself by the fire, you get rid of the effect then go back outside. Now you are going to get cold again. That warm fire solution did not address the cause fully, it only removed the effect. The solution to that problem is to wrap up warmly so your body will not feel the effect of the cold wind when you go out in it again.

Handling an effect (condition) is a temporary measure that fools us into thinking we are cured. Most of our health remedies do not create permanent results because they work on our conditions only.

Now that you know who you are, you recognise that it is YOU who has the ability to think, not some part of your body. So you have to **think** these things out for yourself from now on.

BAD HABITS

We have learned and created many bad habits over the years.

When we try to live using our Mind only, we stop our flow of godlikeness from flowing through our body.

When we rely on the energies found in our Mind only, they gently lead us on a downward spiral to destroying our body. In other words, most of the energies of our past imaginings are responsible for killing the body. The past has gone. It's ended. It's finished.

Those past unpleasant memories are energies that affect

your body in the now, but only when you keep putting your attention on them, only when you keep stating how bad your life is. Think about it. Are you on a murder-go-round or a merry-go-round?

To become god-like using the Mind only, we need other people to back us up and follow our instructions. That makes us feel powerful. Through all this physical material-type support we begin to feel we are at last somebody. The more energy from others we collect, the more powerful we feel we are.

As an example: When a friend decides they no longer wish to be your friend, you may get angry and your body shows a red face. Red energy is blood racing through our body's veins ready to create a destructive action: please don't hit them in the face.

On the other hand your face may turn white. This indicates that your energy has rapidly drained from your body, and you may feel you are not good enough, especially if you have been relying on their energy to make you feel as if you are somebody. Using our Mind method of feeling 'god-like' is unhealthy, and the only thing that can get unhealthy is our body. Your real energy does not need to be boosted up by others for you to be somebody.

Also, light is white, Spirit Realms we class as white light, so a white face is indicating that you need to go into the white mind. Sorry, the Right Mind immediately to talk this situation over with your HS. This is the place where you get a beneficial energy boost.

ANOTHER WAY TO RECOGNISE BODY FEELINGS

As you get to know how your body works from your point of view, you can use the same technique to improve Earth living with others.

Imagine all people as being in the same family, the family of humans. We can learn to do with others what we do with our cells. We can start working with others as a team. It's a much better system than trying to belittle, get rid of or kill those who do not agree with our personal ego system.

If we are working for a firm, and we get to hear they are about to sack a certain department, that information doesn't make any body in that firm feel good. 'Thank goodness it isn't our department', we say, and that brings a smile of relief. But we still have a nagging thought in the back of our mind. How long will it be before it is our turn to go? We dwell on the negative, so we no longer feel happy and secure. Our beliefs about the firm suddenly take a turn for the worse, caused by the imagined feelings our Mind is generating through our negative thinking.

We often fall into the habit of dwelling on the unpleasant side of things. We as Souls start thinking only of ourselves, instead of doing what our cells do, and work as a team.

All those still working for the firm should be working as a team to try to find ways to make sure the firm doesn't slip down any further. We could keep the firm afloat by pooling our ideas. We may come up with some good workable suggestions. This is the way our HS works with us. HS offers us suggestions, so why not apply the same system to the firm we are working for.

BODY WORK - TO SOLVE A PROBLEM

A cell passes to its replacement cell all the knowledge it has gained in its life. The new cell adds to this memory its own experiences as it lives through its life, which again is passed to its replacement cell. This is the way evolution takes place in our body.

To solve a problem, we need to follow another set of evolutionary guide lines. A problem is something that is preventing you from achieving your desire and moving forward.

First accept the fact that you are the Soul in charge of your body. Know and accept that your body is the effect of your problem. You Soul still have the problem.

Do not justify why your body has a problem. That is a way of saying you want to keep it, or that you have not made a mistake. You may say it is someone else's fault that you have it.

■ Go deep inside your body and know you are there.

■ Now go into your Right Brain. This is the light side of your body. Light penetrates the dark, so the energies of your left brain or mind cannot go there. From this place your body relaxes without fear.

■ From this place, penetrate the dark recesses of your Left Brain's mind with your light and find the movie that is causing your body pain and giving you a problem. Your body cannot be the effect of dark energies while you are in the light of the Right Brain.

■ Stay in your right brain and look closely at that movie and find the actions you asked your body to create that caused it pain. Take full responsibility and accept the moving images you are shown as your truths.

- Let your cells do the talking; let them tell you what you said or thought that caused them a problem.

- Now go out of the door in the top of your head to the Right Mind and talk it over with your HS.

- Ask your HS the best way to solve this situation.

- Your HS will suggest a few ways to solve this situation and your body cells who are with you in feelings will choose the method they feel they can do that would makes them feel good.

- Take full responsibility for the physical, mental, or verbal actions you **intend** to create by adding the energy of **desire** to the actions.

Sometimes we ask for help from the HS and do not stay there long enough to listen to the reply, or we do nothing with the reply. We don't follow it through.

Sometimes in life an accident is arranged that forces us to stop and listen to what we are doing. We love to point our finger at someone, or something after an accident. We use a typical phrase like 'It was not my fault'. But an accident never happens on its own. We need to find why we were there and what our part was in that scenario. What is it we needed to learn from that experience?

Sometimes we get a feeling we shouldn't travel on that day, or at that time, or along that route. Your HS always does its best to help you to have a safe journey.

Maybe at that time you were being asked by your HS to stop and think about what you are about to do, or the way you were doing something but you refused to listen. After a period of refusing to listen, a so called 'accident' happened that put you in a position where you had no choice but to stop and think about what you are doing.

Sometimes a matter is so important for you to know that it takes an accident to get your attention.

You see, we often forget or give up easily after asking a question, but our HS never gives up trying to give the answer to us.

Your actions may have been taking you and others down the wrong road. HS could see where you were heading, but will never tell you about a possible future. If it did it would be intruding in your space with the intention of controlling you. You Soul are the Big God on Earth, so HS offers you ways to solve the situation, but you still have to listen and choose which way you intend to go, or create.

RECOGNITION THROUGH THE AURA

As a loving Soul Being your white light penetrates through the vibration of your body's Earthy rainbow colours. The brilliance of your light mingles with your Earth colours and makes those colours lighter. When this happens your light is felt more by others.

When you start acting more as Soul, you may notice your Aura changing colour. You are no longer following a rigid Earth pattern. Ultra colours may appear in some of your chakra areas, depending on which energies you use the most. Green, blue, indigo and violet belong to the Spirit Realm. None of the actions you create using these colours can be seen with your body's eyes because they are mentally created thought actions.

You Soul are resonating all the time, and when your body's energies harmonize with yours, they are sensed by others as favourable or unfavourable according to their reality of life. You do not have to talk to somebody to get to know if you like them or not. When you put your attention on them, most times you know.

Without your body you cannot be seen, heard or known. Only your body has a name, not you. This is telling you how valuable your body is to you. You are only accepted and recognised through your body.

You Soul do not have a name. You are in this world but not of it. Your body belongs to Earth and stays tuned into you, no matter where you go on your 'walkabout'.

WORKING FROM OLD BELIEFS

Person A
Have you wondered why some people talk only about how unpleasant life is? They say everything keeps going wrong for them, nothing ever goes right, they never have any luck, etc.

Person B:
'My life wasn't going too well so I changed a few things. Now it is completely opposite. I just can't do a thing wrong. I love it'.

What did person 'B' do that 'A' didn't?

It is what you do when an unpleasant experience shows up in your life. When something isn't working for you, you look more closely at what you are doing. Find what you are getting wrong.

Start a Q & A on it. Has one of my beliefs just proved to

be false? If I reverse its energy flow, would that make it work? Try it and see.

If you realise that belief wasn't yours in the first place, then you need to get rid of its energy from our body.

Can you remember why your body has an unpleasant feeling? What are those feelings saying to you? Yes! You are not doing something in a loving survival way, maybe towards your body, or towards another. Remember you are a part of Source, you only know love. Maybe you're not showing your love and respect in a loving manner. Only you know the answer to that and the pain is reminding you of that fact.

So which God are you following? Is it an angel or an evil devil? Remember; **evil** is **live** backwards. Are you doing things in reverse, are you creating your experiences as an ego being? Are you showing the opposite side of your Brilliant Divine Self? Again, only you know the answer to that.

Are you trying to be 'Holier than thou'? That is no different from being a 'mischievous devil'. Lies, false truths and negative beliefs cannot honestly make you or your body feel better.

Let's look again at person 'A'. They are wallowing in the mud of past experiences. They are willing to put the blame on anything or anyone other than themselves.

Ah! We may have hit their soft spot. They may *think* they are incapable of doing anything. Maybe this is the belief they are following. So now: **Somebody has got to do everything for them**. That is another of their beliefs. All they are capable of doing is complaining. That is the only belief they are willing to follow. The Law of Attraction kicks in, so they have no problem finding plenty of things to complain about. What a boring life they have chosen to create. They can change that situation any time they wish by following person B's example of looking inwards and taking a good look at what they are doing that is not correct.

Let's look at the way person 'B' dealt with their unpleasant feelings.

They just couldn't understand why they were feeling rotten. Perhaps it's the house I am living in that's causing these feelings? So they go out for a walk to be among nature. They sit down and admire the scenery and notice they feel a bit more cheerful. They start wondering: when I go home am I going to get caught up in those bad feelings again? There must be something I can do! When did they start anyway?

Ah yes! I remember, I was arguing with my best friend in work over something we were trying to solve. His ideas were ridiculous, they will never solve our problem. He wouldn't listen to what I had to say and I know I was right, it was the only way. Why couldn't he see that? I mean, he said we would do it this way, and came up with a crazy idea.

A long pause followed. Hang on a minute… Perhaps it is not such a bad idea. I can see where he is coming from now. Yes it does have possibilities, we may need to adjust this bit a little, and this, and then I think it might work. Perhaps my way isn't the only way after all. Wow wee I *feel good*. I must phone him.

I still can't get over the fact that to a certain degree he was right. My belief 'there is only my way' is not a truth. I can see it now - there could be hundreds of ways to solve this problem, depending on who is solving it. I am going to change my old belief, which is not a truth. I now believe there are many ways to solve a problem.

Now he must rid his body of that old belief.

Find where the pain is in the body. Using your imagination, put an open window with a big sill in the skin where the pain is. Tell all the energies of that belief to leave your body instantly. They will rapidly appear on the windowsill as large colourful butterflies and fly off. They only came into your body because you invited them in with the belief. They hated being in your body, they couldn't stand the light you were transmitting. They spent all their time trying to hide from you. So they don't need a second bidding to leave your body - in seconds they will all be gone. Now close the window and turn it back to skin. This may sound daft, but you still feel the satisfaction and comfort in watching them go.

His awareness when with others had lifted a notch. His attention was then directed to another long-standing problem where he realised he was following a belief given to him by his father when he had been a boy and had just started work.
That belief was never one of his own, so he automatically got into the above procedure to remove the energy from his body. Now he was feeling on top of the world. How come I am able to solve these problems so easily, he wondered?

Then he realized his HS was giving him the information. It only seemed to works when he moves out of the 'Mind' space his problem is in and goes into the quietness of his 'Right Brain'. He realized he can *think more clearly* when he lets the world go. He also noticed that his problems didn't stimulate him into anger when he was in his 'Right Brain's' place of quietness.

He learned that changing his old no-longer-needed beliefs and removing his false beliefs freed him to the point where he could make his life work the way he wants it to. Well, most of the time he could - he didn't always get it right. He tried putting the process on automatic and it didn't work.

You have to be here and do it each time as if you have never done it before. Life can only be created in the now, and you have to be here to create it.

Can you spot Person A's core belief? It may go something along these lines. They were probably told when they were young that they could not do something. They most probably got some simple thing wrong they were trying to learn, like making Mum a cup of tea, but they accidentally spilled it. Over time they got other things wrong, so they changed that belief to 'I can't do anything right'. So look at the nasty mess they have put themselves in now. They feel rotten and always angry, always looking for the next thing that's going to go wrong in their life. They are convinced they can't do anything right. Where has the fun gone in their life?

Our two main faults are the things we do wrong with our body and the thoughts we attach to those experiences and store in our mind Our Body is not the only thing that really screws up our life. Without an active, well-balanced mind we can feel we are worthless.

CHANGING YOUR REALITY - CHANGES YOUR BELIEFS. CHANGING YOUR MIND - CHANGES YOUR EXPERIENCE.

It doesn't take a genius to apply this.

Negative energies have never worked for you up to now, so now is a good time to redirect your thinking power to positive ways of thinking, then you can start making your life work the way you desire it to be.

Remember: we create by first tuning into our imagination's energies. From there we create or look at the imagined pictures we have our attention on; positive or negative, good or bad according to our opinion of the situation we have in mind. We naturally do it thousands of times a day, and it takes a few seconds. We can extend our movies at anytime. The misuse of this ability causes all our problems.

Be in your body and notice if its muscles are relaxed. If not, take a deep belly breath, relax your muscles on your out-breath and be calm.

Sometimes a body tenses for no reason. It's just a bad habit and slows its energies down. The more calm and relaxed your body is the more easily it creates the actions you ask it to do.

LISTEN TO YOUR BODY'S FEELINGS

How many times do you listen to your body's feelings and do something about it when it says it is hungry or tired? How often do you stop eating when it says it is full, or rest it when it says it is tired?

Your body is a tool, a living animal you have made to create your actions. Its health should be your top priority. Without it you have no Earth game to play and that is dead right.

Maintaining your body is more important than maintaining your car. Your car cannot take you anywhere until you put your body in it. Then your body cannot take you anywhere in your car until you tell it where you want to go. Every action comes from you Soul. You are the one in charge of your body's experiences.

ON THE MENTAL SIDE

If that which you have your attention on is not important then let it go. If it is important, then do something positive about it.

Remember, we only play games down here. You Soul have the power to keep a game the way it is, or you can change it if you do not like the way you are playing it.

If you use your **determination,** then nobody can make you play any game differently from the way you want to play it. Some of your games you planned before you came to Earth, so make sure you play them as well.

Does your body like the way you are asking it to play a game? Some games we think up can be quite sickening, can't they?

PLAN YOUR DAY

What do you **intend** to happen today?

If you **desire** to make those things happen, then you need to list the order in which you **intend** your body to create them. Think on the **desired** outcome you want for each action. Plan carefully how you **intend** to achieve each action so it gets created your way. You want satisfaction as your reward.

When you have an unpleasant task to perform, look to see who else will benefit from its completion. Feel happy about benefiting others and do it lovingly for them.

If you are not sure how to do something, **talk it over with your HS** and choose from the suggestions offered. Make this procedure a regular habit. If you think it takes too much effort on your part, then get rid of that belief. It takes more effort to resist than to flow.

I DON'T HAVE TIME TO DO MY THING.

Do you have time to do those things others insist you do for them? Are you their slave? If yes, then ask yourself these questions:

Whose life am I living? Who am I pleasing?

How old do I intend to be before I start living my own life?

Of course it's nice to do things for others, but make sure you do them because that's what you want to do, that's what keeps you in the driving seat.

When creating action, keep out of your Mind and stay in the here and now. Each action you create has many cycles of start, change, stop. While playing your game you gain the most pleasure when you arrive at the stop stages. Not because it is done, but because it is done to your satisfaction.

Reshape your thoughts so you remain in charge of all the games you play in the course of a day. You will always have time to do this, so make your life fun. Don't forget, you are also playing a game with your body when you ask your body to create your actions.

IF DOUBTS AND FEARS POP IN...

Any doubts or fears that come to the surface need to be addressed and handled prior to creating the physical or verbal actions. If you are unable to think of a satisfactory solution yourself, then go into the right brain and talk it over with your HS. Let your body choose the best solution.

GOING FOR A JOB INTERVIEW OR A MEETING

- Why does this meeting scare me?
- Does this fear come from one of my past experience?
- What was it?
- What did I think or say that blocked my progress?
- What did I not learn from that experience, other than to put a blocker on future experiences like this?

You can always find time to learn from past experiences if you have a desire to make progress along a certain line of action.

The real reason you have a Mind is to help you to learn from past screw-ups, so you can make progress. It is not there to block your progress.

If your fear is just an old useless belief you are hanging on to from childhood days and it is outdated, or it really belongs to someone else, if it holds no meaning or value to you for what you are trying to do right now, then you can always release it, then state your new way of looking at the situation as your new belief. Or you can reverse the belief by stating the positive end of it as your new belief.

Remember, life on Earth operates from your **thought energy.**

To make life work your way, you don't have to give in and become a nothing, or another's slave, unless that is the way you choose to play the game. The choice is always yours.

You Soul are in charge of all your thoughts and creations. Your body is the machine you use to create your experiences;

it contains all the feelings connected to your present and past experiences in this life. Both of you 'working as a team' can have fun with any adventure you choose to create.

Maybe when you tried to create an experience in the past, you were not ready for it; you may have needed to learn more about other parts of the situation you didn't know about. You can always ask your HS for this information.

As you become more knowledgeable on the subject, don't let these old beliefs stop you from trying again. You are ready and better prepared now, so go for it. Let others see your determination to achieve that goal.

GROWTH

Everything we do is broken down into steps. In the beginning we learned how to move by crawling. After we achieved that our confidence rose, which encouraged us and gave us a desire to learn the next step in learning to walk, then to run, followed by climbing. Each of these steps was shown to you by your HS to improve your ability in life. The pain your body felt when you got it wrong encouraged you to try a little harder to get it right. You wanted to do it. That's showing your **determination**.

If your next step has been shown to you and you ask 'What if?' then your attention has dropped back in to your Mind again. You are looking at some past time when you tried to create that action and you screwed up, or you're watching another trying to create that action, and formed your opinion about what you saw or heard. There are many ways we form our beliefs, and our mind is always at fault. It shows through the words we say and the actions we create. Our beliefs are very untrustworthy, and are not always the truth.

A 'What If?' comes from a fear in your body. That action was never completed correctly last time. Fear is the proof you never made it work.

So look again at your mistakes and correct them. Otherwise those painful feelings will keep happening. Why? Because that is what your **attention** is on.

Fear is the opposite energy of determinism. Don't live with a fear of getting it wrong. Learn what you need to know, then change that belief to match your gained knowledge. Now live with a determination to get it right.

You can change the energy of any mental picture or movie that exists in your personal universe. You came here to live out the dream you created prior to arrival. You stored that dream in the DNA of the first cell of your body. It's now written in the DNA strands of every cell in your body. It is a part of your personal universe.

Now is the time to get back on track and create those things that felt good and right for you when you were young. You know those things that made you smile and gave your body an energy buzz. Find them and follow each one through, and see where it takes you, now that you have more knowledge of the world.

TIME TO UNWIND

In this book I have explained many of the jigsaw pieces that help to create the puzzle called **Your Life On Earth.** I have explained as best I can how a body works so you know how busy your inner universe really is. Know your body is a massive team of helper cells whose desires are to make life work your way. Your body's cells worship you. And they get upset when you come off your mission.

That plants the responsibility wholeheartedly in your lap.

Your cells can only work for you when you feed them these three life-giving energies:

■ **Oxygen for life:**

If your cells stop receiving pure oxygen they will die.

■ **Earth's energy from Nature - all foods:**

If you stop feeding your body with Earth energies (real food) the cells in your body will lose their stamina to create your actions, stress out, and they will die.

■ **Food for thought from Source:**

If you stop feeding your body's cell knowledge from Source it will die.

These are the three ways we use to break the contract we made with our body.

YOUR BODY NEEDS A BREATH OF FRESH AIR

When breathing through the nose, with some people the oxygen doesn't go much lower than the throat. You can hear it in the way they talk from the throat. Most people get oxygen into their lungs, but even that is not good enough. Look at a new-born baby. Nobody taught it how to breathe, yet you will notice it breathes oxygen into its belly. We only associate the lungs with oxygen, but an intake of oxygen travels much further than that. Our lungs are for pumping oxygen around the body. We think only our lungs collect oxygen. Learn to breathe through your belly. If you think that sounds ridiculous, then try this simple test.

Using a timer, take a normal breath in and sing a single sound out loud until you run out of breath. Notice how long that note lasted on your timer.

Now take a full deep belly breath that lightly presses against your pubic bone. Now sing the same sound again and see how long it lasts this time.

You will notice this way of breathing puts more oxygen into your body. Listen to a baby and make this your new belief: With its little lungs it knows how to send out a long screaming note- doesn't it?

'MY CELLS GET MORE LIFE GIVING OXYGEN WHEN I BREATHE FROM MY BELLY'.

Make this your new way of breathing:

Go into your body and take a deep belly breath, relaxing all your muscles on the out-breath. After doing this a few times see if you can feel a warm or tingly energy running down the inside of your legs to your knees. You may also feel a tingling or warming sensation in your toes. If that didn't happen, then practise - it will eventually.

When the body is in stress it becomes tight, causing the heart to pump faster to counteract this condition. If your heart has a problem pumping blood oxygen and nutrients through tight muscles, then your blood pressure may rises.

A red face when you're angry means there are too many tense muscles somewhere in your body. The best way I have found to relax my body quickly is by:

1. Recognising that I need to calm my body down mentally and physically.
2. Going into the Right Brain. Just saying I am there does not work. Just because I am a Soul Being doesn't mean I don't have to do the imaginary legwork and create the actions. I always have to create the mental actions, every single time. I need to use:
   - **Desire** to go there.
   - **Determination** to arrive.
   - And **Knowingness** to know that I have arrived.

3. From this quiet (no ego chatter) place I can do anything; so again using **Desire, Determination, and Knowingness** I breathe into my lower belly and feel the oxygen lightly pressing against my pubic bone.

4. As I breathe out, I relax every muscle in my body. I do this with **Intention** and a **desire** for this to happen. I feel my body's muscles relaxing as I breathe out and I **know** that I have just done this to the best of my ability. Only I am in charge of my body.

5. I continue breathing in deeply and relax on each out-breath about six times, or until I feel my body is nicely relaxed.

After I have deliberately relaxed my body, its healing systems turn on. I know my heart is pumping oxygenated blood and nutrients into every cell in my body, which it couldn't do when I was physically tense or mentally stressed.

Why don't you try it? If you do nothing else other than get out of this world by going into your body and relaxing it once a day, or more, just to put oxygen into it, then you have started your healing process. As a bonus your nervous system will calm down and your blood pressure should adjust to where it is supposed to be. Your cells know how to control your blood pressure, even though we don't know exactly what is going on. But we do appreciate the calmness and the good feeling it creates.

When you have relaxed your body and you feel quiet and slightly dreamy, this is a good time to deliberately be with your HS.

Your HS is only a thought away, so **imagine** going out a door in the top of your head, to the **Right Mind** and talk to your Higher Self for a while.

Give your HS a small problem you have trouble solving and see what comes back to you.

You are always receiving **inner-tuition** from your HS, so watch, feel and listen out for it. Use the same method you use to listen to the rubbish in your Mind, and believe in your ability when it starts happening for you.

We are not physical beings. We are thinking Souls who live in this 'Moment of Time'. We use our natural projection ability when we are in this corridor of time known as present time. We use this space to do many things, such as looking at and reliving our past, touring Earth, touring space and going to the Spirit Realms to chat with your Higher Self. We can do all these things on a moment's impulse.

Many of your Beliefs need the 3 Rs: Reversing, Reshaping or Removing. Any belief you have that you know belongs to another can be returned to them with your love. But that's another subject.

- Your past is where you go to locate the actions you need to improve upon.
- You move into the Spirit Realm to find the best way to create these improvements with the help of your personal HS.
- Your body cells take this new experience out of 'Thought Form', bring it into your body and materialise it on Earth.
- You ask your body to create the necessary verbal or physical actions so you can also enjoy the new experience you asked them to create on Earth.
- Now is the only time you have to create your life experiences, so use that time well.

PISCES

Through our misinterpretation of the meaning Pisces energies were sending us, we may have set in motion the many war games we learnt to play. From our war games we should have learnt that they were a non-survival game set up by opinionated beings. Killing other Beings is not what we came here to do.

Why do we still buy into and encourage earthbound death games known as 'The Survival of the Fittest', or is it 'Survival of the Thickest'? We can't kill everyone who is different from us.

Do we not realise that our opponents have something very

important to say about their way of living? So why do we try to force them to live our way? Our real enemies are those who will not allow humans to be the way they are. It is in our nature to help those who are struggling to survive in any way we can?

Just because we don't know why some Souls have come to earth, it doesn't mean we have the right to kill them. Thank goodness our mistaken power of Pluto has come to an end.

It will take us a while to clear up the debris.

Aquarius is now sending us knowledge to learn new ways. We Souls have a better game to play now called 'Survival of All'. This includes the Earth we play on and all its life forms.

SLAVES

A Slave is somebody who does for us the things we cannot be bothered to do for ourselves. On Earth we may become a slave, or we may have a slave of our own if that is our desire.

In the Spirit Realm, everything is perfect the way it is.

The idea of having or being a slave to another does not exist.

We are all gods in our own right - we don't need a spirit slave.

No Spirit Being is willing to be your slave. That idea opposes the purpose of being a God. If you walked through a muddy puddle, would you ask God to clean your shoes for you? Yet we often ask God to do things for us which we are quite capable of doing ourselves.

WORKING THE SYSTEM

Some people want to know all the details before trying something new. They may have trouble thinking for themselves, while others just desire to try the process the way it is. I have covered both types in this book. Only you know if it works for you, the same way it works for me. I hope you make many changes in your life for the better by using all or some of the information here.

THE FINAL WORD

The source behind all illness is in the mind. True long-term healing is not possible unless we remove the discordant energies residing in our minds.

Be aware of your Self at all times. Your natural normal flowing energy is to love everything and allow everything to be the way it is. That doesn't mean you have to agree with everything. We are all different.

Negative Energy (Neg-E) that resists your flow of love is known by many names, such as: discordant – negative – blocking. It upsets the life energy flow in our body. This causes the unpleasant mental, emotional and physical feelings we call pain.

Negative Energies, when we bring them into this here and now moment, cause dis-ease and illness in our bodies, because they are flowing against our natural loving energy.

Our memories are stored somewhere in the DNA strands of every cell of our body, and our cells record every second of our life concerning things that happen in the outside world around our body and those things that happen inside our body.

When we remove Neg-E from our body we do not need to know the exact spot it comes from. When you notice a pain has gone, know and believe it has been released from your body for ever.

The Neg-Es you have kept your attention on for a long time are the energies that are causing your body the most problems at this present moment in time. If you continue to keep your attention on them without removing them, they will continue to make your body weaker and weaker.

To change this situation you need to find and remove the cause. The cause is always a memory away. When the cause has been found and released from your body, your body starts to heal. It knows how to heal itself. By just knowing, believing and trusting that it can, it will. It is built to survive.

How many of your minor conditions vanish overnight? No drugs or herbs were applied, they just went. That's the power of your body's healing ability.

An Earth reality on this:

If a battery in a torch loses its power, the bulb dims. The same applies to you and your body. If you keep your attention on negative experiences, your energy runs down, your light dims, you lose your power and your body gets weak emotionally and physically. You came here to play the game of life by using a body, but when you were shown how to live life backwards, you no longer followed the rules of life. You started moving in the direction which leads to an early death for your body. Why?

When you stop playing the game of life, you have no reason

to remain on Earth's playing field. You Soul never die so your last request is – stop the world, I want to get off.

Let me put **'Your Game of Life'** another way:

When we make a mistake in the game of life, our personal HS shows us a movie called 'The Errors of Your Ways'. The purpose behind this is to allow you to look at your mistakes again so you can gain more knowledge of how to correct your errors, so you become a wiser Soul.

But we did not do that. We preferred to point the finger at others and blame them for screwing our life up. What a big ego we built for ourselves. From that point onwards we no longer play our original game in life. We changed the rules to suit Earth living.

If a football player doesn't follow the rules of the game, if he prefers to kick the opponents instead of the ball, then he is following the rules of his own reality, so he gets sent off the pitch. The same applies to us when we choose not to follow the guidelines of living lovingly with others. We remove ourselves from the game by slowly killing our body so we can leave this playing field called Earth. If we don't want to play the game properly, then when our god 'Money' no longer supports our life, there is no point in staying on the planet.

YOUR NEW AWARENESS

The Source of all Creation is a space in the Cosmos that holds all the knowledge we know nothing about. We could call it the Brain of Source, but that I feel is not the correct wording. It is more like the Source of the Loving Life Pulse.

Now that you know who you are, there is nothing stopping

you from returning to the place of knowledge you used when you were young. There is nothing stopping you from going to that space above the clouds to collect any information you require that will make your Earth experiences more pleasing for you.

You will always need help from your Higher Self, who knows which shelf contains the information you're after. This ability has always been there and was never denied you.

You forgot who you were due to pressure put upon you by Earth Beings who insist you live an Earth life style that suited their reality only.

The energies brought to your attention in this book help you to get back on track as a 'mini god' in your own right. They teach you how to take control of your body, and how to use it in a loving manner. When you create anything on Earth, don't forget to include how it can benefit others as well.

It doesn't matter if learning to be in charge of your own life is a new experience for you or not. We all make mistakes when learning something new, so confine your actions to doing small things around your living space to start with until you get the feel of doing it. Then you can accept the fact that you do have the ability. Every action your body creates is an experience. Make it well known to your Self over and over again that it is YOU Soul who is asking your body to create these actions, not some unknown Entity somewhere in outer space, or some idiot with a big mouth in your mind.

This will create a completely different way of looking at life and the way you think, which I am sure will feel strange at first but pleasing. You don't have to talk out loud to tell your body what you want it to do. Neither do you need to go over the top when you thank your body for creating something for you. You're not going out-of-your-mind. Er - yes you are! You're getting saner. It helps to make living more real for your body.

This is why I say you should apply it to simple, everyday things around your house first. When you feel comfortable doing these simple things and know you are who you say you are, then gradually put this idea into practice in all your activities, one step at a time. Accept it as your new way of living.

Your confidence will build; you will feel more secure and capable. You may realise you do things faster when you take your time. You feel good knowing you are 100% in charge of all the actions you get your body to create. This is the only body you have the right to control. All other bodies you must learn not to control. Allow them to be the way they are (including children). Help them when they ask for help, or you feel they urgently need some assistance with what they are trying to do. Rely on your body's feelings and your good judgment at all times.

BRINGING IT ALL TOGETHER

You as Soul are reaching up to infinity, to the place where you came from. There is nothing as high or as peaceful as this place you know so well.

Your body is an Earth animal. It contains all energies needed to help it survival. That includes you.

Your job is to teach this body to live from your higher level of awareness, which contains no animal instincts of mistrust or envy, while accomplishing your mission for being here. Both you and your body are on a permanent learning curve.

It is through your ability to clearly differentiate between a spiritual (not religious) way of life and an animal existence that makes it possible for you to turn Earth into a heavenly place for you to live. As you are a part of 'The Source of All Creation', you have a rightful place on Earth as the 'Source of your own creations'. All Spirit beings from above accept this fact and offer you assistance in the way of helpful suggestions only.

If any of your Spirit friends, or those who have made contact with YOU, try to tell you what you are to do on earth, or the way things are to be, then know they are not spirits from above but from below. Spirits from above know all things are possibilities. Nothing is solid on Earth until you have created it or until you have agreed it has been created.

Forceful spirits have chosen to remain on earth for reasons of their own. They may try to live their lives through you. They are used to controlling, and wish to continue their evil disguised way of living through you. This is the reason why I choose to follow my HS only.

Should my HS bring another Spirit into my space connected to what I am trying to create, I accept that that Spirit specialises in the subject I am having difficulty with. Spirits do not have names; only their information should interest you. People often want to know who they are talking with so they can brag about who they know. But knowing will not help your situation in any way.

As Soul you have the ability to distinguish what is good and what is bad through the team work you have created with the cells in your body. It is their *feelings* that talk to you. This is how you get to know which animal instincts still need educating in your body.

Your conduct and body's emotions should always recognise the situation in front of you. Drive away eviL and welcome the good in others, no matter how poorly they present their good to you.

CREATING POSITIVE BELIEFS

Imagine you are about to start a project and it occurs to you that you might fail. It also occurs to you that people may think you are stupid for trying. Can you see how those two beliefs will prevent you from trying?

If you had the belief that the project were going to be a total success and people would acknowledge you for the quality of thought you put in to the project, those beliefs would spur you on.

Why do we choose to give our desire a negative meaning, when we want people to think well of us? What is wrong about being successful? Who or what takes over our life when we desire to be our Self?

The answer is two emotions called '*Fear*' and '*Failure*'. We have been taught from a very young age what happens when we get things wrong. We have been taught how painful it is when we do not do as we are told. Any idea of being your *Self* is not allowed in the system.

We feel we cannot be as good as those who have controlled us all our lives, so when those two negative energies show up in our mind together, they create a *Fear of Failure*.

It is much easier to look at and surrender to the negative side of life than it is to take the plunge and make a life successful by adding new dimensions to it. Most of us choose the easy way out because we have been taught and brought up to believe that being controlled is the ONLY way to live.

There is something you have to do to make your life work the way you want it to. Now you know who you really are, you need to apply a little more force by adding the energies of **Desire** and **Determination** to your idea so you make **Your life** works **Your way**. Get angry about it – you are not harming anyone.

Allow me to explain how we fell into the trap of our modern way of living.

Our ancient people used to honour and worship false Gods. Through fear, they took them offerings in order to stay on the right side of these gods. Everybody wants to survive and live well.

About 1,400 years ago somebody decided to bring God down to earth and use it as a religion for their own benefit. These religious people were the only ones who were allowed to speak directly with God, as the rest of us were sinners. So in our innocence we used to tell these religious people what we thought were our sins, through a fear of not going to Heaven. As awareness grew these religious people became wise men and found businessmen who offered them money to grant them forgiveness and to keep them on the right side of god. Who knows what shady dealings these business men had with the public?

As time passed, governments learned from the churches how to extract money from working people. This was no longer a free offering given by the person but a demand from our leader. They called it a tax. You see, with our ancients it was an offering made by people, but when money also became our god, it changed to a demand by the leader. They said the money was needed to enable them to protect us and look after us. Eventually our leaders forgot the god bit. Our churches have turned into bingo halls and other recreational places, and our leaders have taken over the role of being in charge of the people and money themselves.

Can you see that when we follow Earth ways only, we gently move further and further away from the plan Source created for us? Over the past 2000 years, we have learned how not to live life on Earth.

A child takes a little while before its brain is fully formed. Then past experiences start sinking into its mind and it realizes it has made mistakes as stated by others.

Earth time and space time are different. Space time goes by in a blink of an eye. Your trip to Earth is like a week's holiday according to space time. Earth time slows time down, so you have ample time to learn a lot of lessons.

Our old way of living has ended; our new way of living has started. We will live between the two ways until we become capable of working out a harmonious way to live with each other.

You knew this was going to happen before you came here, that's why you choose to come to Earth at this time. Your reason for being here and what you do is important for all of us. Your mission for being here will come back into view when you start removing your negative beliefs.

Let us now put all the pieces of this jigsaw puzzle together in a workable order.

BEING POSITIVE ABOUT YOUR LIFE

Before you can do anything, you need to bring yourself back into your body. Only from there can you successfully get your body to create the actions you desire for others to see.

GROUNDING

1. Get back into your body and know you are there. Relax any tense muscles you become aware of. Breathe deeply through the nose into your belly area until you can feel a slight pressure on the pubic bone. Breathe out through the mouth and relax all your muscles.

   Do this a few times until you know your body is completely relaxed. Continue gentle belly breathing. Your body cells love the extra oxygen you are giving them.

2. Now your body is relaxed, move into the right brain and know you are there. From this place you can view a past experience of your choice without being the effect of any emotional energy connected to it. Your left brain contains a large wave of information suited to Earth's heavy energies. Those energies cannot get into the right brain, which contains only the energy of LOVE. This wave looks more like a fine straight line. As Soul you can move through material objects like walls, but your body can't. As Soul you can pull out memories from your left mind without bringing the heavy effect energy with them.

3. Prove what I say is a truth for you. The trick is to make sure you are in and that you stay in the right brain as you dig out from your mind a mildly unpleasant experience that recently happened in your life. You will notice you are still clear and relaxed in the head and body. You are looking at that movie without being the effect of it.

4. See if you can think up a solution that will solve that problem and make everyone happy. If you are successful, then put that solution into action as soon as possible after this demonstration, to complete its cycle of action. You will also feel much better after doing so. If you were unable to find a solution to the problem, then be imaginative.

5. Use your Imagination - it is a valuable tool. Your Higher Self is in a space just above your head - wherever you say it is. Go out of the imaginary door in the top of your head and be with your HS. It happens instantly. All your life you have travelled using your imagination, so doing this is nothing special. But knowing you Soul are doing it is very special. It puts you Soul back in charge of your life.

6. In thought form, talk your problem over with your HS and ask how you can solve this situation. You will be shown in movie format a variety of ways that match your reality level to solve the problem. With your eyes closed you will see these movies, one at a time, in front of you. As you watch these short movies, one of them will make your body feel good to do. This is the cells in your body talking. They are saying which way they would like to create the action.

7. When you are happy with the method your body cells intend to use to solve the situation, bring that movie out of the world of possibilities and give it to your body to create. This operation takes place through your right brain only. This is pure energy and is not contaminated by your left brain's mind of the past.

Know that you are killing a false belief that only what you see on Earth is real. Everything you see on Earth was first created by someone using their imagination. They went to the place where reality comes from, which I call 'The Source of all there IS'. The information you require is given to you with love.

With practice you should feel pleased being reconnected with your HS. It's been a long break, so rejoice, you're back home again.

DANGER

Never go into your left brain to get answers to your questions. In that area you are 100% controlled. From there you will find how weirdo imagination works. It is a world of crazy make-believe, full of nonsense and false truths, as vividly displayed to those taking drugs.

REMOVING FALSE BELIEFS

It takes us seconds to form a belief about anything we see in our space and everything our body feels about what is happening in our space.

We create beliefs *mentally* and *emotionally.* The energy installed in our beliefs affect the cells in our body when we have our attention on its subject.

This means you may be the effect of a belief for the rest of your life. The energy of a belief is the information you Soul chose to believe, and it is passed from the old cells to their replacement cells. Belief information is your personal awareness of Earth living and forms your personality.

Beliefs that do not help you to live your life in a loving, friendly, flowing manner are opposing your purpose for being here. This means their energy is flowing in the opposite direct to the way you intend to live. To be rubbed up the wrong way is always a painful experience *felt* by and in your body as pain.

As far as your cells are concerned *this is a painful experience and is causing your body dis-ease.*

These Negative beliefs are know by other names, like blocking energies and dark energies: They didn't want to come into your body, but you invited them in when you accepted a belief given to you by another without proving to yourself that what they told you was a truth, or they came from your own belief also not checked out as a truth. All untrue beliefs are dark energies. The dark finds the light painful, so as you are the light in your body it tries to hide, and this causes havoc with your cells.

REMOVING DARK ENERGY

To remove a dark energy you need to put your **Imagination** to good use:

1. You have to accept that this dark energy is there, in your body.

2. Create an imaginary window in the skin where you feel the pain, and open it. Make sure there is a wide sill on the outside. If you feel no pain in your body, create the window between your navel and your ribs.

3. You need to use your imagination to do this. Ask the dark energies attached to your problem to leave instantly and watch them move onto the window sill like jet-propelled caterpillars. They turn into beautiful butterflies and fly off.

4. Know that they have all gone and that you have completed this action. Now close the window.

5. Your body will start its own healing process, which may take a few days to complete, because your body belongs to Earth and is controlled by Earth time. Just believe you are your own healer.

If changing a belief; accept the new belief first, then send out the dark belief and your personality will improve. This process has to be done to each negative belief you want to remove as you become aware of it.

You have sufficient information to start making your life work your way.

Don't be the same tomorrow
If today made you feel blue.
Make a Decision for tomorrow
TO BE - A DIFFERENT YOU.
Right now, put fun back into your life
And make your dreams come true.

A NEW AWARENESS STORY

I had just finished proofreading my book, sent to me by my publishers, when I received the word in my head saying HS. Yes, I thought. So what, long pause and nothing else said? What was I missing? This happens to me sometimes when I am with a client. I feel their energy is preventing me from tuning into my HS properly.

For some unknown reason, If I go up stairs to the loo room everything becomes clear again and my questions get answered. So off I went to the loo. The word HS came over again, then - *as above so below.* Was I having one of my thick moments, I wondered? Yes, HS is the one I trust. What has that to do with Earth? Hold on! I've got it. My body on earth doesn't have an HS, it has parents! No I haven't got it yet. As I was walking downstairs trying to get my head around this problem, it came to me. **As above so below.** The parents of a human body are not its HS, they are its guardian. So as above so below doesn't apply here. When that child body has matured into an adult it moves off to do its own thing. **As above so below** – So we Soul don't have an HS either! We did not leave some part of our Self in Spirit realm to help us out. We are here on earth as a complete energy unit.

OK - I see my mistake now. Why didn't you tell me this when I started this book? You wouldn't have understood, you needed to gain all this knowledge before your EGO would accept the word Guardian. I thought I had got rid of my Ego! Ego was built into your body by Source, you had trained it to your new way of *thinking;* you have stopped it from flaring up at the wrong times, but it's still ticking away in the background, it has other jobs to do you know nothing about. It needs to flare up quickly when danger is about. OK, I believe that. I can hear it now, purring quietly in the background.

In your *mind* please change the words Higher Self and HS to *Guardian.* In a strange way the word Guardian *feels right*; it makes me feel more comfortable, more secure than using HS. How about you?

THE BEGINNING